"ONE BOY'S DINNER PLEASE."

Memories of Life and Work in Edinburgh
1942 to 1974

Alan Bews

"ONE BOY'S DINNER PLEASE."

Alan Bews

Memories of Life and Work in Edinburgh
1942 to 1974

Edinburgh Tenements

Artist: Lindsay McCrea

Author: Bews, Alan.

Title: "One boy's dinner please": memories of life and
               work in Edinburgh, 1942-1974 / Alan Bews.

Publisher: Moorooka, Qld.: Boolarong Press, 2008.

ISBN: 9781921054167 (pbk.)

Subjects: Bews, Alan.
               Ferranti Ltd.--Biography.
               Trade unions--Scotland--Officials and employees--
Biography.
               Edinburgh (Scotland)--Biography.

Dewey Number: 331.88092

 Boolarong Press
Publishing your dream

Unit 1/655 Toohey Road, Salisbury Qld Australia 4107
www.boolarongpress.com.au
Typeset by Boolarong Press, Salisbury, Qld Australia 4107
Printed and Bound by Watson Ferguson & Company, Salisbury, Qld Australia 4107

Contents

Preamble..vi
Foreword...viii
Dedication for my Grandchildren x
Abbeyhill Area..xi
Chapter 1 1
Chapter 2 3
Chapter 3 6
Chapter 4 9
Chapter 5 13
Chapter 6 18
Chapter 7 24
Chapter 8 29
Chapter 9 34
Chapter 10 40
Chapter 11 46
Chapter 12 52
Chapter 13 71
Chapter 14 79
Chapter 15 84
Chapter 16 89
Chapter 17 92
Chapter 18 95
Chapter 19 98
Chapter 20 102
Chapter 21 108
Chapter 22 111
Chapter 23 113
Chapter 24 117
Chapter 25 119
Chapter 26 124
Chapter 27 126
Chapter 28 130
Chapter 29 132
Chapter 30 134
Winter-time...139

Preamble

I was asked by my daughter-in-law, Soraya, to write a story of my life in Edinburgh so that my grandchildren would be able to relate to Edinburgh life at that time. My wife Roslyn, sons Graeme and Stephen, and daughter-in-law Tiffany were all supportive of the idea and encouraged me to do so.

Because of my upbringing I was reluctant to openly discuss family business; as a youngster I was always told to keep such things 'in the family'. Showing off and being 'full of oneself' was also discouraged. On balance, and after much soul searching, I decided to go ahead with my story.

I have tried to include my memories of Edinburgh as it was during my earlier years growing up in Abbeyhill, and later during my time as convener of shop stewards at Ferranti, right up until my departure to Australia with Roslyn and the boys in 1974.

It is not a complete history of the Bews family as such, as I do not have enough details of the family history, but it is basically the story about my life and some of those who were part of it.

I have not asked permission from those whose names are prominent in this story, but hope, as they are mostly written about in a positive manner, that they will not be offended or embarrassed by its contents. Names of non-family members who are mentioned in a negative way have been changed to protect their identity.

I have spent much time considering if I should include Chapter 8 which deals with my mother's decision to help her father in his time of need. I have decided to include this chapter. As, whilst it may have been easier to leave it out, it was a part of my life and I feel that I owe it to my mother to include it. However I am not critical of anyone involved during this period as it would have been a very difficult time for all family members, and I hope that after so many years no-one will be overly upset about this disclosure.

Foreword

This is a precious book, not only to those who know Alan Bews personally (his family in particular, for whom it has been written and who will surely treasure it), but also to anyone interested in Edinburgh during the period he writes about; the three decades or so immediately following the Second World War.

Edinburgh today is a very different place from the city of Alan's early life. Many streets, including Alva Place, may look the same, but there are lots of modern additions, like a certain well-known building at Holyrood! However, the way of life has altered enormously because of things like television and the computer, and, I suppose, the general economic and social changes which have taken place. Things which fundamentally affect the experiences of young people growing up in school and at home and in the neighbourhood, and then when entering the world of work. While much of this is welcome, by no means is all of it. The disappearance of many things that feature large in Alan's account of his upbringing and development is greatly to be regretted, because much that is rich of human character and of real community value has been lost. This is what makes this book a precious record.

The story is beautifully told. It is the product of an amazing memory for detail; a capacity to assess with great honesty and discern significance objectively, for all the memories are intensely felt and held with obvious fondness; and the ability to recount these memories simply, vividly and at times with the narrative tension of a good play which has an unexpected ending. Reading it, you find that you want to know what's coming next and what the outcome of the problems encountered will be, and you stagger at the tragedies, which indeed might have been more than a lesser person than Alan could have overcome so well.

The qualities of this book come from the qualities of the man. I was lucky enough to come to know Alan well over the years when I was minister of the church in Edinburgh's West Pilton, beside which Ferranti's main factory was situated. We grew close and I came to admire him greatly. Together with a rare talent for trade union leadership, which had he remained in his native country might well have taken him to the very top corridors of power in British industry, Alan combines the qualities of selflessness and compassion which eventually made him realise that his life with Roslyn and the family should be in Australia. Such is the admirable character that emerges from this fascinating account of the author's life and times.

Colin Anderson
June 2007

Dedication for my Grandchildren

"Be confident and honest to yourself and others, and take your opportunities in life."

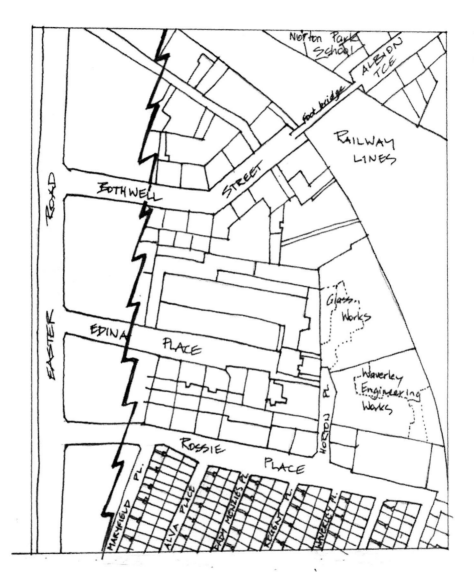

Abbeyhill Area

xi

Chapter 1

I was born at home at 15 Alva Place, Abbeyhill in Edinburgh on October 18th, 1942 at 5.30 in the evening. My father's name was Arthur Trevelyan Fairgrieve Bews named after his mother's father; he was employed as a railway engine stoker. My mother was Janet Elizabeth Bews, formally Janet Elizabeth MacKenzie. She was a dressmaker prior to her marriage. I was the second and the last child in the marriage. My brother David James MacKenzie Bews was born four years earlier on September 29th, 1938. I weighed 10 pounds, 7 ounces at birth and was carried in a wicker basket from my parents' small bedroom into the kitchen/living room for all to see. My brother remembers the day very well as it was the day he says that he ceased to be the centre of attention.

My parents were married on the 15th of January, 1937 - my father was 27 years of age and my mother was 33. They were married at the Registry Office at Hillside Crescent, Edinburgh and my father's friend and fellow railway worker, Alexander Bickerton, and my mother's sister, Donaldina MacKenzie, who were later to marry and become my aunt and uncle witnessed the marriage. The wedding was in some ways a sad affair as the reception was cancelled due to the illness of my father's parents who were both down with pneumonia. My father's mother died the day after my parents' wedding, and my father's father died seven days after that; both within a week of each other. Both aged 63 years. On reflection, the sad start to the marriage was an omen for more heartache and sadness in the time leading up to my mother's untimely death at the age of 49.

Whilst I never met my father's parents by all accounts they were very decent people who raised eleven children in a tenement at 36 Parsons Green Terrace, Edinburgh. My grandfather, Thomas Bews, was a brass finisher by trade, and it was a coincidence that I started my working life as an apprentice brass turner at 15

1

years of age with James H Lamont at their Gylemuir Works, Corstorphine.

My father's parents were married in Edinburgh on the 30th of December, 1892. My grandfather, Thomas Bews, was 20 years old and prior to his marriage lived with his parents on Blackfriars Street, and my grandmother, whose maiden name was Isabella Fairgrieve, was 19 years of age and lived at 160 The Cannongate. My grandfather's father was called Frank Bews and he too was employed as a brass finisher. His wife, my great-grandmother, was called Louise Gaffney prior to her marriage. My grandmother's father was a housepainter called Arthur Fairgrieve and her mother's maiden name was McDonald.

My mother's parents, particularly my grandmother, were to play a big part in my life. My grandfather, James MacKenzie, was an engineer's timekeeper and my grandmother, Jessie Bryce MacKenzie, whose maiden name was Macdonald, raised four children; my mother Janet, her sisters Donaldina and Teresa, and her brother James. They lived in a very small tenement house on the ground floor at 10 Rossie Place, Edinburgh which was a five-minute walk from my home at Alva Place. My grandfather's parents were Duncan McKenzie who was employed as a gamekeeper in the Highlands, and his wife whose maiden name was Cameron. My grandmother's father Donald McDonald was a Mole catcher by occupation and her mother's maiden name was Ritchie.

Chapter 2

Alva Place, in the suburb of Abbeyhill, is a row of housing built by The Edinburgh Cooperative Building Company which built much of the 'colonies housing' in Edinburgh. These 'colonies' were built to provide housing for the many workers in Edinburgh during this period. Colony housing houses were not tenement flats which had common access through a front door and stairs. Instead each family had its own very small garden patch leading to its own front door.

Our neighbours above had their front door entry in the street behind us at the top of a stone staircase with iron railings and we looked out onto their garden patch from our kitchen. Our family lived in the ground floor house which consisted of a kitchen, a bedroom, a box room which was a small storage room and a parlour as well as an indoor toilet. The upper floor house was similar except it had two extra bedrooms. Where as in a tenement, on entry you walked into the main living area, in the colonies housing the kitchen was separated from the parlour which was the main room.

Abbeyhill was one of the older parts of Edinburgh which I believe took its name from the ruined Holyrood Abbey. The Abbey was built in the year 1128 and its remains still stand in the grounds of Holyrood Palace.

My parents did not own their Alva Place home but rented it for the princely sum of approximately 12 pounds per year. It was not common at that time for working class families to own their own homes. In fact, the rent was almost perpetual because under legislation, owners could not remove people from their homes if they paid the rent as per their rental agreement. Even after the death of their parents, a son or daughter could continue to rent the premises if they wished to do so. Twenty-three years after my father's death, I decided to continue living in the house much

3

to the disappointment of the owners who were keen to regain the control of their property, but who were unable to do so because they had no legal right to their property as long as I wished to stay there.

Alva Place was a short walk to the St Margaret's Railway Shunting Yard at Piershill where my father worked. It was a working-class area not far from the city centre and very close to the Royal Mile, Edinburgh Castle and Holyrood Palace. The whole area was steeped in history and it was not unusual to see the Queen and other royalty during visits to Edinburgh as they were being driven from Waverley Station, down Regent Road, and past the Regent Cinema to their Scottish Capital residence at Holyrood Palace.

There was a good cross section of industry in the area around the time of my birth. The famous Edinburgh Crystal factory was only a few minutes walk from my house, and I have fond memories of sneaking into the factory with other boys during school holidays and playing hide and seek and cowboys and indians around the cardboard boxes and packaging in their yard. It all came to an end when one of the workers would catch us and chase us for our lives. Thank goodness it was the 1950's when security guards and dogs were not needed to protect a companys premises and people generally took a more liberal view of youngsters growing up.

I also remember the workers from Miller's Foundry on London Road walking from the foundry at dinnertime - some off to the pub and others to Oldham's the grocer who had a small room at the back of his shop where he used to serve dinners from Monday to Saturday. It was very basic and, if you were lucky enough, you could get a place at the table and a chair to sit on. There was also a number of school kids from the local schools who used to go to Oldham's for dinner, which we would now call lunch break, for one of Oldham's famous 'boys dinners'. There were also a few pensioners as well who, if I remember correctly, used to pay a bit less for their meals.

Years later, when I was a teenager and worked after school and on Saturdays as a grocery boy at Gunn's on Easter Road, I used to eat at Oldham's at lunchtime on Saturdays and during school holidays. The food was cheap, old fashioned and very well cooked by a lady who we never saw in a kitchen downstairs. I only ever tasted their boy's dinners once. It cost me four pence and it was a plate of potatoes and peas with a ladle of gravy poured over the top. My favourite things to eat at Oldham's were their soups and apple dumplings, as well as their famous pie dinner, which was an individual meat pie with potatoes and vegetables served with a thicker, better-quality gravy poured over the pie.

Scottish Brewers was a bit further down the road from Alva Place and every time I drive past the Fourex Brewery in the Brisbane suburb of Milton, it reminds me of the smell of hops and yeast coming from the Scottish Brewers brewery as I walked down the lane at the back of the Regent Cinema on my way to play at King's Park.

King's Park, which during my time was also called Queen's Park, as the name changes depending on the gender of the current monarch, was a large tract of parkland in which there were a number of football pitches surrounded by hills and the famous Salisbury Crags and Arthur's Seat. Holyrood Palace, which is situated at the bottom of the Royal Mile, looks out over the park which I understand is now called Holyrood Park. Another well-known landmark that looked onto the park was the Elsie Ingles Maternity Hospital where our first son Graeme was born in 1972.

Chapter 3

As I have mentioned, I was born at home in my parents' bedroom, a small room off the kitchen/living room. The house was small and the only other room in the house was the parlour, which was eventually to become a bedroom for my brother and I; the parlour was traditionally a room which held the family's better furniture. It was used mainly for guests who would visit and for special family occasions. In our house there was a toilet but no bathroom and for many years I did not have the luxury of a proper bath. Because of a lack of baths in homes at this time it was not unusual to see small children, framed by their front window, standing in their sink being washed by their mother.

I can remember sitting in a tin tub in front of a roaring coal fire as a youngster being washed by my mother, and later as a teenager going off to the Leith Victoria or Infirmary Street baths for a swim and a hot shower. On special occasions I would have a private bath at the local swimming baths and, for a reasonable price, luxuriate in a bath of endless hot water washing in red carbolic soap and drying myself with a large white towel courtesy of the Edinburgh Town Council.

During the first few months of my life I contracted pneumonia and was so ill that I was taken to the Royal Infirmary. There my parents were advised that I had a dangerous amount of fluid in my lungs, and that it would be touch and go as to whether I would survive. The surgeon decided to operate and cut into my left side inserting tubes to extract the fluid. This action eventually saved my life but left me with a nasty scar. When I eventually left the hospital, the matron told my mother that because of my illness and the operation I would never pass the medical examination for conscription into the army when I would turn 18 years of age. I never got the chance to test out the matron's theory as conscription was abolished in Britain a few years before I reached the age for National Service. As it transpired, the illness had no effect on my future life and I made a full recovery with the scar on my side being the only reminder of that difficult period in my young life.

Other parts of my early life are difficult to remember although I do recall standing in my cot, which was positioned to the side of the fireplace in the kitchen/living room, and my father handing me a chocolate Santa Clause. It must have been Christmas morning as there were Christmas decorations hanging from the walls. It would have been early in the morning, around five o'clock, just before my father left for work. In those days people in Scotland worked on Christmas Day but had New Years Day and January 2nd as official holidays. It was many years later before Scotland recognised Christmas Day as an official holiday. I can remember working Christmas Day as an apprentice brass turner; it was always a very slow and boring day as people wished away the hours until they could rush home for their Christmas dinner of chicken, brussels sprouts and plum 'duff' (pudding) and celebrations with their families.

During our early years, my brother David and I always hung our pillow slips up at the end of our bed on Christmas Eve, and then we would try to get to sleep as soon as we could so that morning would arrive more quickly. Morning could be as early as five o'clock and we were never disappointed even if our pillow slips were only made fuller by including an apple, an orange and a mandarin which was always wrapped in silver Christmas paper. I always thought this silver paper made it a bit special.

There was always great excitement as we ripped open our presents trying to make as little noise as possible so that we would not wake our parents. Back then Cadbury's chocolate selection boxes or a large chocolate Santa was a prized inclusion in our pillowslips and were usually all eaten before eight o'clock. Other Christmas favourites often included were comic book annuals. I can still smell the freshness of a new *Beano*, *Broons*, *Dandy* or *Roy of the Rovers* Christmas Annual as my brother and I turned over their crisp new pages, devouring their new stories and jokes. We were an average working-class family and large presents were never expected or received but we were never disappointed with what we were given.

Chapter 4

Alva Place was a safe and happy street to grow up on as a child. The street had steps at the top of it, making it a no-through road and a safe place for children to play. And, as there were very few motor vehicles around at that time, children were able to spend their days playing on the street without fear of incidents. I seem to recall that I spent most of my summer days playing outdoors; dressed in my light blue dungarees and sandals as my mother and brother watched over me to ensure that I did not wander off somewhere.

It was during that time that I became fascinated by the road sweepers (scaffies) who would regularly come to our street to brush our gutters clean. Perhaps it was the fact that they also wore dungarees that led me to talk to them all. By all accounts I became well known to the local scaffies as I followed them down the streets with my little broom, cleaning up behind them. My brother would often have to come looking for me to bring me home.

Perhaps it is only my imagination, but the summer months I experienced in Edinburgh as a young boy seemed so much warmer than the ones I experienced as an adult. The days were warm and, in the height of the summer, it did not become dark until near nine o'clock. During those summer months, it was often difficult for mothers to get their children back into the houses to do their homework or get ready for bed. Mothers would often roam the street looking for their children who would be playing oblivious of the time, or perhaps hiding irrespective of it.

In the summer, local boys would gather to give the work horses buckets of water to help keep them cool. It was not unusual to see groups of boys standing around as the horses drank their fill. The boys would then gasp as the horses urinated into the gutter with great force and flow. The younger boys would run down the gutter trying to keep up with the speed of the urine as it disappeared down the siver (drain), to great applause from the older boys.

Winters in Edinburgh were icy cold. And my memories conjure up images of people throwing cooking salt down the snow-lined streets to melt the snow and ice and make it easier for people to shovel it away from their doors and pathways.

In winter, the coalman would visit our house with his Clydesdale horse, delivering our coal. The coalman's muscular Clydesdale would struggle to keep its hooves on the ground, doing its best not to slip in the snowy conditions. On these occasions, my mother or brother would take me out to feed the horse a slice of bread. I would offer the bread with an open palm and place it directly under the horse's mouth. I can still feel the delight of the horse's wet lips and the snort of hot air as it skilfully scooped up the bread, and the relief as I realised that it had left my hand still attached to my wrist.

The coalman's visit was always a highlight for me as he had to enter our house to deliver our two bags of coal. As I stood with my little hand holding onto a kitchen chair, I would be mesmerised by the coalman; six-foot tall, built like the side of a house and as 'black as the ace of spades' from the coal he would carry into the house on his back and the coal dust that would fall around him during this task. Our coal cellar was situated under a trap door in our kitchen/living room floor and my mother would pull the carpet aside and lift up the door to allow the coalman to dump his heavy load into the cellar. You can imagine the cloud of stoor (dust) caused by this, and after the coalman had made his messy delivery, my mother would set about scrubbing the floors and cleaning the house. Within an hour the coalman's visit and the dust he spread were only a memory. But I would eagerly await his return, and that of his horse.

On reflection, I can see that those Clydesdale horses played a big part in helping the Scottish economy develop. Pulling heavy carts of goods in the years before trucks and lorries became affordable to local business people. There were still many horse-driven carts around Edinburgh during the 1940s and I took great delight in watching the workmen and their carts deliver various merchandise; fruit and milk and kegs of beer, as well as bags of coal. My only disappointment now is that I'm unable to remember the names of the various horses that delivered their wares around the streets of Abbeyhill. I would have fed most of them, or stood and patted them by the side of the road as they chewed their dinner of oats from swaying canvas bags roped around their necks and muzzled under their mouths.

Another memory of those winter days is the soot. A by-product of the coal that we burned in our fireplace, soot would build up in our chimney and if it wasn't cleaned out it would make it difficult to start the fire in the morning: smoke would become trapped in the chimney and eventually bellow backwards into our living room and kitchen instead of escaping up through the chimney and into the air outside. I am sure that my mother would not have looked upon the visit of the chimney sweep as the highlight of her day but I always found it exciting. Initially, the chimney sweep would try to dislodge the soot by pushing his brush up into the chimney, and if that did not work, he would then climb up onto the roof and push his long brush down our chimney to clear away the build-up. The soot would then drop into the soot bag that he had placed in our fireplace below.

Our next-door neighbours were Mr and Mrs Elder who lived at number 16. Almost 30 years later, Mrs Elder was to become an unexpected benefactor to me: I shall explain this in more detail later. I was to become close friends with Mr and Mrs Elder, although this was not so during my early years of life. My brother and I were always getting into trouble by making too much noise while playing in our garden or by kicking our football into their garden. I always seemed to draw the short straw in having to go and ask for our ball back, which we did not always receive. But it was comforting to know that it would eventually reappear in our garden a day or so later.

Mr Elder was a bit of a character. He was a small muscular man whose first name was George but everyone knew him as 'Dodd'. He had spent some years in the army in one of the Highland Regiments and was quite a tough little character who had a quick temper when roused. Although he did not seem to have any trade background, he was a jack-of-all trades who could turn his hand to most tasks. He also enjoyed a drink and was secretary of the annual bus-trip day, which was organised for the regular patrons of the 'Artisan' pub by the owner, Tommy Curran. The trip was organised for one Sunday each summer and the men would go off in their hired bus with the luggage compartment filled with cases of beer. One can imagine the scene upon their return at eight o'clock as the occupants of the bus emptied out in various states of inebriation.

As a youngster I would lie in my bed and listen for their return. I could always tell when it had arrived by the noise of the happy and tipsy travellers. My father was one of those tipsy travellers who never missed the Artisan 'day out' as he called it, and by all accounts it was a great day for everyone.

Mrs Elder was very different to Dodd. Even at an early age I could tell that she was a little bit different from the other women in the area. She was very self-assured and always walked straight with her head held high. I have a picture of her and my brother David walking on the beach at Burntisland on a day out she had organised. She loved tending her garden as well as looking after her beautiful dog Prince and her cat Jackie.

I believe her father had been in business and owned a lemonade factory and as such she may well have had private means. And although Dodd and she were as different as chalk and cheese, and with no children of their own, they were as happy as Larry in each other's company.

Chapter 5

At five years of age I was enrolled at Leith Academy Primary School. Leith Academy was a fee-paying school and was situated at the foot of Easter Road. It took about twenty minutes from my house to the school by bus. Years later, I would walk to school and spend the bus fares on sweets (lollies in Australia).

I remember my first day of school; my mother and I took the No 1 bus, which we caught at the top of Easter Road. I was all dressed up in my new uniform; a blue cap with the Leith Academy badge, blue blazer, grey shirt and shorts, blue and white striped tie, black shoes and of course my new school bag. By the time we reached the bottom of Easter Road and began walking the short distance to the school I began to realise that I did not like the prospect of being separated from my mother to begin my new life as a little schoolboy. By the time we reached the school gates I had decided that I did not want to go into school. The tears were flowing freely as my mother explained to me that I had to go in then she took me firmly by the hand and walked me along with a number of other children and their mothers into the year one classroom. Eventually, after a very friendly and understanding welcome from our teacher Miss Davidson, she left me sitting at a desk with tears still flowing and feeling totally abandoned.

Miss Davidson was a lovely lady. She seemed old to me at the time, but looking back she was possibly only in her early fifties. She fussed around us all and chatted non-stop. She told us how much we would all love school as we got to know each other and started to learn to read and write and find out so many new things. There were both girls and boys in the class and little did I realise on that first morning that we would all be together for the next seven years.

Two things stand out from my first morning in class. The first was the bottle of milk we received not long after our parents left. We were told that we would be given a small bottle of milk each morning, which we were expected to drink. Milk was never really a drink that I liked very much and to be given a bottle at our morning break on the first day was more than my little mind had anticipated. As we all sat drinking milk through a straw and eating our little 'pieces' (similar to morning tea or lunch food), which for me was jam and bread, I began to feel sick as the warm milk and my piece of bread and jam began to bombard my stomach. I never recovered from this beginning and as a result always used to dread our milk break as the teachers would chastise me for not drinking the full bottle. As I proceeded through the school years some teachers were worse than others in trying to get everyone to drink their milk and whether the milk was curdled because of the summer heat or frozen in the winter chill, we were still expected to comply and drink it.

The second thing that sticks in my mind was the square sand tray and stick which was used instead of paper and pencils to copy the letters of the alphabet from the blackboard. We used the stick to trace the letter out in the sand. Learning to copy the letters into the sand on that first day highlighted that I was different from other kids; I used my left hand to hold the stick as I tried to copy the letter. I could not understand why Miss Davidson was so concerned, but for the next year or so she, and other teachers, tried all sorts of techniques to get me to write with my right hand. The end result was, that despite all their attention, I never did learn to write with my right hand. On reflection, being a 'lefthander' singled me out in the class as being different from my other classmates and I am sure that it had an effect on my confidence during the early years when I was learning to write.

I don't recall when my mother stopped taking me to school in the mornings, but I assume that it was after I had settled in. After that my brother would haven taken me as he was four years ahead of me and one of the so-called 'big boys' at the school. I know that at the beginning of my school life I always felt better knowing that David was at the same school, I suppose that at that young age of five I felt more secure knowing that he was around.

We used to come home at lunchtime for lunch, which was then called dinnertime; our evening meal was called teatime. I would trail behind David on the way home as he would always keep me at a distance, he walked faster than me at that stage anyway. I remember that I was a bit of a dreamer and I would walk down Alva Place trying to catch the bluebottle flies in the palm of my hand as they rested on the walls of the houses on my way home.

Dinner on a Monday was always soup and pudding as it was a washing day and it took my mother most of the day to wash the clothes by hand. The soup was usually potato or lentil or scotch broth. But my mother, who was an excellent cook, also used to make a lovely barley soup. She would put milk in the soup to cool it for me so that I could eat it quicker as we did not have a long dinner break. Puddings were also a treat. My favourites were jam roly-poly, apple dumpling and rice or semolina, and rhubarb. For the rest of the week we would get a main course and pudding and I can still remember, as a little boy, sitting down to rabbit pie, rabbit curry, Irish stew, and mince and dough balls to name but a few dishes. And when she could get the main ingredients of condensed milk and sugar and butter, which were rationed during the Second World War and shortly afterwards, she would make wonderful tablet which was a traditional Scottish sweet.

A few years later, whilst I was still at Leith Academy, I used to wonder why I was sent to a fee-paying school as almost all of the children in my area went to the local school in Abbeyhill. Although we were not a well-off family, my father's job as an engine driver would have paid more than the local tradesmen and was probably slightly above the average working-class wages. I recall taking the money to school in an envelope when the fees were due. Years later, when I spoke to my father about our time at Leith Academy he said that it was my mother's wish that we went to a fee-paying school and that if it had been his decision, my brother and I would have attended the local school.

My mother was a gentle person but could be firm when the occasion demanded. I can still remember when she caught me and some very young friends playing on Easter Road, we were running across to the other side of the road in front of oncoming cars. I guess it would be the equivalent of playing 'chicken' in today's language. It must be said that this was in the 1940s when cars were few and far between and did not drive at fast speeds. Nevertheless, my mother took me firmly by the hand - in front of my pals (the Scottish equivalent of mates) - and, to my embarrassment and with some trepidation on my part, dragged me along to my grandmother's house and into the bathroom where she smacked my bottom as I yelled out in pain and, I assume, some hurt pride. She explained afterwards why she had punished me and I never ever played 'chicken' again. It was the first and only time that I recall my mother ever smacking me in that way.

Another experience that is etched in my memory was when I went shopping with my mother to the local St Cuthbert's shop on Easter Road. St Cuthbert's was a co-op of members and when you purchased your goods from them you received a cash dividend half-yearly or quarterly. It was a popular way for working-class people to buy goods economically, and also receive a dividend payment. In our family this was always welcome. I can still remember sitting on the counter as my mother ordered her goods. I would have been about four or five years old – or perhaps a little younger – when I noticed a box of liquorice allsorts on display on the counter. I suddenly thought it would be good to have a box of those and proceeded to slip the box into my mother's bag unnoticed. We then went around to visit my grandmother, I handed over my non-purchase to a flabbergasted mother and grandmother. After a long lecture about honesty and how thieving was the lowest of the low, especially from your fellow-man, and woman presumably, and after being threatened with the 'Bobbie' - the Scottish nickname for a policeman - I was taken back to the store where I handed back the liquorice allsorts to the woman at the counter.

My mother was a regular churchgoer until she took ill. She attended the Abbeyhill Church of Scotland church, which was at the top of our street. The minister's name was the Reverend Broadfoot. He visited our house on occasions, which was a part of his duties and at these times if I saw him walking down the street towards our house I would make a quick exit. I always perceived the Reverend Broadfoot to be very stern and authoritarian. Similar to most of my pals, I tended to view visits to our street by the minister to be associated with sickness or death, or even worse from a little boy's perspective, being caught missing out on Sunday school or the Cubs. I was baptised at Abbeyhill church and still have my Certificate of Baptism. The church has long since been demolished and the site used for housing.

When I was old enough, my mother enrolled me in Sunday school, so for a few years I would make my way up the road on a Sunday morning to attend the Abbeyhill Church of Scotland Sunday school. I believe my mother's brother and sister, Uncle Jimmy and Aunty Terry, also attended church; they were both accomplished singers and sang in their respective church choirs. I remember going with my mother to hear Aunty Terry sing solo at her church on Easter Road and she was very good indeed.

I don't think my mother was in the church choir but must have been musically inclined as she still had her old violin at home. She used to show it to me but did not play it. My mother's family must have been interested in music as I recall my grandmother having a piano, which I am told my Uncle Jimmy could play, in the parlour at their Rossie Place home. My brother David received piano lessons from Aunty Terry but that did not last too long as he lost interest.

Chapter 6

As a young boy my father was a distant person to me as he always seemed to come and go at different times and seemed to sleep at odd times. It wasn't until later that I understood the meaning of shift work. He worked night shift - 9pm to 5am, day shift - 6am to 2pm and back shift - 2pm till 10pm, five days per week, Monday to Friday. The only time we would sit as a complete family for dinner would be during his day shift or on the weekends if he was not working extra shifts. As I grew older I used to listen for him coming home from night shift. My mother was usually up by then and, if it was wintertime, would have the fire burning. My father always brought home warm, well-fired, crusty rolls from MacAinsh's local bakery on Easter Road. At that time of the morning, when he finished work, the rolls had just been baked and were as fresh as the morning dew. He would cut up the rolls and spread salted New Zealand butter all over them and the butter would be slowly melting as my brother and I would head towards the table. I can still remember the feeling of peacefulness and pure satisfaction as we sat around the breakfast table devouring the hot, crusty buttered bread rolls and drinking our mug of hot sweet tea beside the roaring fire whilst outside the winter wind and rain would buffet our windows. The joy was short-lived however as we eventually had to go out and brave the Scottish elements to make our way to school.

My father was a member of the NUR -The National Union of Railwaymen - which represented a wide range of railway workers and some engine drivers. When he joined the railway he started work laying railway lines as a railway worker and joined the NUR but he did not change to the ASEF - the Amalgamated Union of Engine Drivers and Firemen - when he became a fireman and eventually an engine driver. As a youngster I was always confused when the NUR called a strike for some industrial reason and my father went to work, but when the ASEF called a strike he would support the strike and stay at home. He believed in the principle of trade unionism but whilst he was not active in politics or the union, he did take an interest in both. Sometimes, when we were out walking, we used to stop at the Mound, a type of speaker's corner beside the Scottish Art Gallery in Princes Street, and listen to the various speakers who were mostly communist and those with left wing leanings, as well as some extreme religious fanatics. In my later life discussions with my father, I came to the conclusion that he felt there was more chance of working people getting a better deal through trade unionism than through the Labour Party. His view, which I did not share, was that the Labour Party was better in opposition as he felt they kept the government, the Conservatives, honest.

My father's other great passion was for the Heart of Midlothian Football Club. He was a great supporter of the Hearts and on occasions he would travel to see them play outside of Edinburgh when they played their away games. Fortunately it did not cost him anything to travel to these games because, as a railway worker, he was allowed a certain amount of free travel passes each year.

The Hearts were founded in 1874 and were affectionately known as the 'Jam Tarts' by their supporters. Their home pitch was at Tynecastle Park at Gorgie and their club badge was based on the heart shaped mosaic built into the pavement near St Giles on the Royal Mile which marked the site of the old Tollbooth Prison. Tollbooth prisoners used to spit as they entered the prison and even today some people spit on the mosaic as they pass.

I am told that at the outbreak of the First World War Hearts players enrolled for active service which gave a lead to others to support the war effort. There is a memorial to the club at Haymarket in memory of the sacrifice of the players and the club during the war years.

The other major football club in Edinburgh was the Hibernian Football Cub which was, and still is, the Hearts' greatest rival. They were founded in 1875 and their home pitch was at Easter Road Stadium. They were formed by members of a local Roman Catholic Church from the Cowgate and were supported by members of a large Irish Catholic population at that time; the club's name reflected its Irish roots.

I came to reflect that women from working-class families had a difficult life during the period around the 1940s; bringing up the children whilst some husbands spent their time following their football team, drinking, smoking and gambling. Fathers were seen as the breadwinners, which seemed to give them the right to gamble on a Saturday afternoon and then go out to the pub for a drink with their mates on a Saturday night.

My father was a heavy smoker and he did like his daily bet and pint of beer at the local Artisan Bar. On a Saturday evening, when the pubs closed at 10.00pm, he would always bring home fish and chips, which the Scottish call a fish supper, from Bald's on Montrose Terrace. He and my mother would share the fish supper and, if my brother and I were still awake, they would bring us some chips on a saucer.

Gambling with street bookmakers was illegal during my younger years, but this did not deter people from placing bets with them as they hid in stairways always on the look out and one step ahead of the local policeman. When I was 13 or 14 years of age, my father used to get me to put on a bet for him if he was working. I used to love the excitement of looking out for the policeman at the same time as trying to find the bookie I was to place the bet with. I still remember the name of this bookie; he was 'Big George' and his father, who was an ex-amateur boxer, owned the business. Big George was a happy-go-lucky fellow who was also an ex-boxer although not a very successful one by the look of his broken nose, which seemed to be spread over most of his face. I used to lie in bed some nights wondering what would happen if my father won a substantial amount from his bet and Big George did not pay up. The thought of my father (like most small boys I thought my father was invincible) fronting up to insist on payment from Big George used to fill me with horror. However my over-active mind need not have fretted as most street bookies paid out winnings especially Big George and his dad who were known for their honesty.

My father also liked the music hall type of theatre and I recall going with my parents and brother to see a few shows at the Empire Theatre. I recall one of the 'turns' when the 'Top of the Bill' was Winifred Atwell who was a black pianist famous for her big smile and honky-tonk style. Years later, after my mother died, my father would take me to see some of the great Scottish comedians such as Lex McLean, Chic Murray and Jack Milroy at theatres in Edinburgh such as the Palladium and the Gaiety in Leith. These comedians were not sophisticated and were very working-class in their approach to comedy, but they were all very talented and could sing, dance and play musical instruments as well as make you laugh. They all worked very hard with two shows a night from Monday to Friday and, if I remember correctly, only one show on the Saturday evening, and each week the show would change to a new format. I loved my trips to the theatre with my father as we always left the theatre full of admiration for the comedian and still laughing at their jokes. Lex Mclean was my favourite comedian, he was very successful in Glasgow where he, "packed them in" at the Glasgow Pavilion year after year. He was a great supporter of the Glasgow Rangers Football team and when he was playing in his show in Edinburgh it could be a riotous Saturday night in the theatre if the Rangers had beaten the local Edinburgh teams as he would bait the audience during his stand-up comedy at the start of the show.

I can remember going for family walks on a Sunday afternoon. My father and mother seemed to enjoy these outings, probably because it was one of the few occasions apart from the occasional trip to the theatre or family get-togethers that we were all together. My favourite trip was taking the bus to the terminus at Fairmilehead and walking up on to the Pentland Hills, which was a range of hills on the outskirts of Edinburgh. From there we would walk to Swanston Village where the well-known Scottish writer, Robert Louis Stevenson, spent his childhood summers recuperating from ill-health away from the Edinburgh climate. The house still stands today, it has a thatched roof and I believe is now owned in trust by the City of Edinburgh.

The highlight on these Sunday afternoon outings was the ice cream my brother and I would have as our mother and father sat in a café having a cup of tea. I remember on one of these afternoon walks we had a bit of excitement when we came across two teenage boys who were fighting and intimidating a smaller boy who was crying. My father ran up and chased them away and then we walked the smaller boy back to the bus stop where my father gave the boy a three-penny bit for his bus trip home as the older boys had taken his money.

I also looked forward to our family gatherings on Christmas Day and New Years Day. Prior to my mother's illness, my parents would take turns with other family members at having the family over for a party. It did not bother me where the party was held as it was always a great occasion for everyone especially the children. I well remember parties on New Years Day at my fathers sister's house at Corstorphine. Aunty Bella and Uncle Charlie always made everyone welcome and the food was typical fare for Scottish New Year; I always enjoyed the home-made beefsteak pie with mashed potatoes, brussels sprouts and home-made beetroot. The pudding was normally a trifle and home-made apple pie, and of course there was always the obligatory black bun and shortbread. Alcohol was also in abundance but over the years I only remember people being jolly and happy on these occasions with singing and laughter being the only tell-tale sign of alcohol consumption.

All the children were encouraged to sing a song or tell a joke; I used to sing a song as during my early years at Leith Academy I had joined the school choir and enjoyed it immensely. Another reason I liked to sing was that you always received some money as a bribe to encourage you. This could be as little as a three-penny bit or half-a-crown depending on the amount of alcohol our uncles had consumed on the night. I also loved to listen to the adults singing. My father's sister, Aunty Ada, always sang *Danny Boy* and even today, after all these years, when I hear the song played I remember the parties and the happiness and the sense of belonging they brought to my life. Aunty Ada's husband, Uncle Alec, was also a good turn on these occasions and his party piece, *Hawick's Queen of all the Borders,* was always a highlight. Uncle Alec was a good friend of my father's and in the years after my mother's death, I became very close to him and Aunty Ada and my cousin Moira, as well as with my Aunty Bella and Uncle Charlie and cousins Ella, Charlie, Katherine and Marilyn.

One of the best parts of these parties for me was sitting under the table hidden by the tablecloth and drinking the dregs of the beer bottles which were invariably placed at the side of the table when empty. After completely emptying the bottle I would use a knife and pull out the cork from under the lid of the bottle. I would then place the cork under my jersey at chest level, press the bottle top onto the cork through my jersey then, by the end of the evening, I would have a row of coloured medals on my jersey from the various types of beer drunk that evening.

At the end of the evening we would make our way from the party to the bus stop and wait in the freezing cold, and in some cases snow and frost, for the last Number 1 bus of the evening to come to take us back home to Alva Place and a nice warm bed.

Chapter 7

During my early years my mother was a big influence on my life and being the youngest child I was very close to her and she was very protective of me. It was not until my mother died from breast cancer when I was nine years old that I got to know my father better. I grew very close to him during the years prior to his death. He died fourteen years after my mother, at age 57, from leukaemia.

I don't remember too much more of the time between starting school and just before my mother took ill. My life during these years would have been similar to that of most boys my age. I seem to recall that I was not doing very well at school possibly because I was still under pressure from the teachers to stop writing with my left hand, I recall this was a big issue each time I got a new teacher.

My mother's family of Aunty Doll and Aunty Terry never seemed to come to our house very often but I did see them and my cousins at my grandmother's house from time to time. Years later, when my brother and I were older, Aunty Doll and Uncle Alec Bickerton kept in touch and made sure that we were included in their happy family gatherings and at the weddings of our cousins Maureen and Joan.

I do recall spending a lot of time with Aunty Terry's oldest son George. She and I would take him for walks to the lawn bowls green at Montgomery Street and around their home at Gilmerton. Aunty Terry and her family eventually immigrated to Canada.

My mother's brother, Uncle Jimmy, was married to my father's sister, Aunty Minnie, and they lived in Oxford and eventually South Africa. When they were living in Edinburgh, between emigrating to South Africa on two occasions, they were, because of Aunty Minnie, close to my father's family and attended most of the Bews' family functions.

My grandfather McKenzie, who could be cantankerous at times, tended to frighten me a little. He was well known around Rossie Place as the man who occasionally took his cat for a walk on a lead. I do remember on one occasion seeing him with the cat on a lead with his walking stick whirling in the air as he tried to chase away some small children who were following him to get a closer look at his cat.

If my grandfather was cantankerous at times, his cat Toby was ten times worse. He only had one good eye as a result of frequent fights and had also lost some of his fur and what was left was dirty and unkempt. He was most unfriendly and his welcome was always a hiss so people tended to stay clear of him. I cannot remember ever talking to my grandfather very much as he believed in the old adage that adults were to be respected and that children were to be seen and not heard. I remember walking with my mother to the Northern General Hospital on a bitterly cold December evening to see my grandfather; he was ill with complications from diabetes and thrombosis. He died a few days later on December 16th, 1949 at 72 years of age.

I never really understood how ill my mother was in the year or so before her death. I did notice that Doctor Ferguson began to make house calls to my mother. Unbeknown to me, my mother had developed cancer of the breast. During her illness, life did not seem to change as she still looked after my brother and I almost up to the end. I did notice however, that she became very tired and looked very much older than other mothers but I was too young to realise how ill she was.

It was about this time in my life that we got a new schoolteacher. I was not doing well at school, and on reflection, my mother's health must not have helped my schoolwork. My father would say, "He is no brain box, but he is a good boy and that's what matters".

Our new teacher, whom I shall call Miss Temper, was a tyrant. I was in the bottom five or six in the class and the seating structure was that the best students sat at the back of the classroom and the less gifted sat progressively towards the front. I always sat in the first or second row and was always, along with some others, the butt of some cruel remarks from Miss Temper. She was a tall rigid women with white hair pinned into a tight bun at the back of her head. What did not help me at the time was that I was getting special lessons in writing in what the other students used to call the backward class. On reflection, I don't think Miss Temper was impressed with me leaving her class to go to the backward class as she probably felt it was a reflection on her. I have to say that Miss Temper terrified me and I was always disappointed when I saw her erect figure walking along Leith Links to the school in the morning.

Apart from ridiculing some others in the class she was also prone to screaming at me and smacking me on the back of the head. I remember once when she asked the class who the Prime Minister was I quickly shouted out, hoping to please, "Churchill Miss". She retorted, "Mr Churchill, you horrible boy".

I can't recall when my mother took to her bed prior to her death, but I don't think it was for a long period. I remember sitting in her small bedroom at home talking to her, but I think she was being heavily drugged with painkillers and not always aware of things. I do recall that there was more activity in the house and I assume now that family were around to support her and my father.

It was around this time, at a school morning assembly where we all had to wear white shirts that Miss Temper noticed that I was wearing a shirt which I had worn before. As she passed me, she looked at my shirt and lambasted me for wearing a dirty unironed white shirt. Her shrill voice created somewhat of a spectacle for the gathered assembly and I could feel the unwelcome stares from my fellow classmates burn through me; this only made my sense of hurt and embarrassment even worse. I remember breaking down and telling her that my mother was ill, but she did not seem to care and went on ranting. Fortunately some of the other teachers came to my aid and things settled down.

After my mother died, my father visited the school and spoke to the headmaster and things improved a little. Not long after that Miss Temper collapsed in our class from a burst appendix and never returned to school. Our replacement teacher, Miss Aitken, was surely an 'appointment from God'. She was a wonderful person and a very good teacher.

My mother died during the night at the age of 49 on the 1st of June,1952. That next morning, my father came into our bedroom to tell us that he was sorry but our mother had died. He told us that we would need to stick together and make the best of it as it would not be easy on our own. That morning, after breakfast, our father gave my brother money to take us both on a bus trip, possibly to get us out of the house as funeral arrangements would have had to be made. We took the bus, which was a double-decker, to the Sighthill terminus and just sat there looking out into space as we waited for a bus to return to Abbeyhill. Later that day, as I sat with a friend on the kerb outside my house, the undertaker turned up with my mother's coffin. My friend asked me who was dead and when I said it was my mother, he quickly jumped up and ran away. The sight of the coffin really jolted me as I realised for the first time that I was going to be different from other children as I would not have a mother to run home to and that my life would never be the same again.

My mother was dressed and laid out in the coffin in her bedroom until her funeral; this was the way it was done back then. It would have been difficult for my father to shield us from all the talk and the emotion of the next few days. I believe, although I can't really remember, that we would have gone to stay with our grandmother McKenzie just around the corner at Rossie Place until the funeral.

As was normal at these times, there was a short service around my mother's coffin in the parlour of our house. This was conducted by the Reverend Broadfoot from my mother's church. The parlour was crammed full of family members including my mother's brother, Uncle Jimmy, who had travelled from Oxford to attend the funeral and comfort my grandmother. My grandmother was unable to attend the funeral as she was housebound due to an ulcer on her leg.

After the service in the house, everyone made their way to the crematorium at Seafield where there was a big turnout of people who came to say their goodbyes and pay their respects. Afterwards, the families made their way back to our house for some food and refreshments; it was only then that people began to relax a little. It was during this time that my father and Uncle Jimmy agreed that David and I should travel to Oxford for two weeks to have a holiday and spend some time with Aunty Minnie and our cousins Sheila and James.

Chapter 8

It is appropriate at this time to fast forward five or six years to enable this part of my life to be understood within the context of my mother's life and death.

If I recall correctly, my father and I were sitting in our house watching television. I remember it was a Sunday evening. I would have been either in my last year of school or when I was just starting my apprenticeship as a brass turner; I would have been fifteen or sixteen years of age at that time. My father began cautiously and slowly with carefully chosen words. In retrospect, he spoke in this way so as not to upset me too much, as he would not have known what my reaction would be to the story he was going to share with me.

As I was told, it happened that my mother's father had been embezzling money from his employer and that, unknown to my father, my grandfather's employer had threatened him with the police and jail if he did not repay all the money. My father believed that my grandfather had used the money for gambling or alcohol and that neither he nor my grandmother had the money to repay the debt. Fearing jail, which he may not have survived, my grandfather must have pleaded with my mother to help him. As my mother was very close to him, she reached a written agreement with my grandfather's employer that she would pay back the embezzled amount in instalments. With this unselfish act, my grandfather escaped jail. I can't recall the amount of money involved or how long my mother had been paying the debt back, but it must have been a few years as I believe the theft had been found out not long after my grandfather retired.

My father first became aware of this when, a day or so before my mother's funeral, he went to his wardrobe to check his suit and found it missing. As he searched the house for his missing suit, he found other items missing and pawn tickets with which to retrieve these items. My mother had hidden these in various places around the house. Shortly after my mother's funeral, my father was contacted by my grandfather's employer to pay back the outstanding balance of the debt and he refused. He did not hear from them again.

It would have been hard for anyone to have understood my father's feelings at this time. He had just lost his wife and was left with a big challenge of bringing up two boys on his own. And on top of that, was the revelation of the pawn tickets, the missing items and a debt which he had no prior knowledge about. As he talked to me on that evening he showed no bitterness but told me that he could not understand how my mother could have sacrificed us as children and him as her husband as the money used to pay off the debt was taken from the housekeeping budget. He said that on reflection, he had noticed that the food was not as good or as plentiful, and that my mother was always struggling to make ends meet even though his wages were always slightly higher than those of other workers at the time. He also said that he should have discussed the household budget with my mother at that time, but that as she was in the early stages of cancer, he put the problem down to my mother's illness and decided to let it pass.

My father said that after my mother died a small number of people contacted him about money my mother had borrowed from them. His biggest worry at that time, was the number of people who may have given my mother money and who did not, because of her death, bother to claim it back. He also said that he knew that people would have been told through word of mouth about my mother's sad story and may have assumed that he did not give my mother enough money to run the house. The fact that people may have thought badly of him was just another burden he had to carry in the months after my mother's death. I could never imagine how my mother would have felt, as she approached her death, knowing that the payback arrangement would become common knowledge after she was gone. The

30

feeling of guilt she must have had must have been almost as unbearable as the thought of leaving two small boys to face life without her.

As my father related the story, I recalled an occasion months before my mother's death when we were walking home one afternoon and she remembered that she needed something from our local shop. Being young and silly I started to run across the street without money. My mother shouted at me to come back for the money and running back towards her I shouted mischievously, "Don't worry, I'll get it on tick" (credit). My mother almost exploded and grabbed my upper arm. She told me never to let my father hear me talk like that. I didn't understand then how my little joke could have upset her so much as it was so much a way of life in working-class Edinburgh at that time, but I can now.

When my father finished telling me the story, my thoughts were that my mother would have been torn between her immediate family and her father. I can only assume that she felt that my father would not have agreed to pay back all the money to the detriment of our family and she must have been aware, or thought that, her brother and sisters would not have taken any responsibility for their father's action; or maybe she did not tell them to protect her father. Her closeness to her father would have made it impossible for her to live with the thought of her father being imprisoned in Saughton Jail, or to bear the stigma to her family name had my grandfather been exposed. I believe that what she did was in many ways heroic and unselfish, and if people believed that she was wrong in doing it, then she certainly paid a high price for her goodness and decency.

That night was the last time my father and I ever talked about my grandfather and the embezzlement. I, for my part, never mentioned it again to anyone, preferring to try to erase it from my memory and no one else ever mentioned it to me. I only discussed it many years later with my wife Roslyn after we had moved to Australia. I have no reason to believe what my father told me was untrue, although I'm sure that there might be aspects that I would have forgotten or was never made aware of, but I now relate the story truthfully as it was told to me.

Perhaps it was because of all of this that my father only visited my grandmother on Hogmanay - midnight on the 1st of January. On this night, my father and I would walk around to my grandmother's house at Rossie Place and, as was the tradition in Scotland on New Years Day, my father would bring a bottle of whiskey and pour out a glass or two for my grandmother and himself, whilst I contented myself with a small glass of green ginger wine. My grandmother would prepare boiled ham sandwiches, shortbread and black bun, and there were always mandarins on the table, covered in the obligatory silver paper.

Since my mother's death I had become especially close to my grandmother and shared my time living between her house and mine. She suffered from a leg ulcer, which would never heal and as such she was permanently confined to her house. I was her message boy and not only did I get all her provisions, but I also used to 'run up the street', as she called it, with a brown paper bag containing a small empty brandy bottle and some money to get it filled for her. She liked her nip of brandy, did my grandmother. And although it was not legal for a boy of my age to purchase alcohol, she must have had an understanding with the grocer at Dryburgh the Drysalters as I never had any problem getting the brandy. My father would give me money at least once a fortnight to take to my grandmother for looking after my brother and I and it was always around that time that I would get the brandy for her.

My grandmother was my refuge after my mother's death. She was always there with food, warmth and comfort even although she just sat in a big chair beside her fire for most of the day. She was, in many ways, as important to me as I was to her.

I used to look forward to the Hogmanay meeting between my father and grandmother; I secretly hoped that it would lead to more visits from my father but it never did. The visit would only last thirty minutes or so and they would talk about the New Years Day Football Game to be held later that day between the Hearts and the Hibs as well as any other news. At the end of the visit my father would slip a pound note into my grandmother's hand and say goodbye to her for another year.

Over the years as I have thought about the terribly sad story of my mother's predicament and her actions, I could see only her humanity and goodness as she grappled with her decision and making it in favour of helping her father. And whilst she spent the last few years of her life protecting her father - and my grandfather - at a great cost to her, I feel that after so many years, her sacrifice should be recognised even if by doing so I reluctantly expose my grandfather's indiscretion. My father never showed any malice or severe criticism towards my mother, nor did he try to undermine my mother's family or my relationship with them. He related the story to me as though I was entitled to know the background, but it was never couched in such a way as to make me take sides or to be unnecessarily judgmental. Perhaps he was concerned that if I found out later and had not been told the complete story by him, that I would have thought less of him as a person. I am glad he shared this story with me.

Chapter 9

There was much excitement at Waverley Station on the day my brother and I waited for the Flying Scotsman to leave for London. It had only been a week since our mother's funeral and, as had been arranged between my father and Uncle Jimmy, we were now making our way to London where we would be met by Uncle Jimmy who would then take us onto Oxford. I loved steam trains, especially the well-known ones such as the Flying Scotsman, the Heart of Midlothian and the beautifully shaped and colourful Kingfisher. The atmosphere was magical to me; I was filled with excitement and yet nervous at the same time about travelling as far away as London on our own. I was glad that I had my big brother with me as he was the boss and would look after me.

Most of our relatives were at the station to see us off. I can still remember my father carrying our cases onto the train and finding us a good window seat. Aunty Bella arrived late with a big bag of chocolate crispy cornflakes made with honey and raisins and held together in little white paper cups. We also had sandwiches wrapped in greaseproof paper inside a paper bag to eat on the long journey to London. This was my first real train journey and it gave me a lifelong love of trains. Once the train moved off and settled into its long journey to London, I decided to look around and left my brother to look after our cases. I was surprised at the number of carriages on the train and loved the power of the engine and the gentle rocking as the train progressed on its journey.

Even as a young boy I understood, albeit simplistically, the difference between first class and third class on trains. The rich, and those who could pay, used first class and the working people, and the less well off, used third class. The class system was alive and well and flourishing in Britain at that time of my life. I was intrigued by the buffet car where third class passengers could buy tea, lettuce and egg bread fingers, and cheese and tomato sandwiches. Some people even drank coffee, the smell of which was foreign to me at that time. Some men stood drinking beer in the rolling carriage managing not to spill a drop. I loved the smell of the carriage and I remember feeling so grown up as I stretched up the counter to order a packet of Smith Crisps and pay the man serving me.

But whilst I was intrigued and fascinated by the buffet car, I was totally enamoured by the dining room carriage in the first class section of the train. As I looked into the dining room I could see white linen tablecloths and waiters doing silver service for people sitting in fine suits and dresses eating what to me looked like wonderful food. My first thought was could I ever afford to eat in such splendid surroundings?

I can't remember much more of the journey to London, but I do remember my brother and me arriving in London and carrying, or dragging, our cases along a very long platform whilst being bustled by other passengers. We walked towards the ticket collector whilst looking out for our Uncle Jimmy who met us once we cleared through the gate of the platform. From there we made our way to another platform to take a short train journey to Oxford.

When we arrived at Oxford I could not help but think of the difference between Edinburgh and Oxford. Oxford seemed so bright and clean; it was technicolour to Edinburgh's black and white. We met Auntie Minnie and our cousins, Sheila and James, upon our arrival and our cousins quickly showed us around their house. I can't remember if the house was a bungalow that stood in its own ground, or whether it was a block of two houses that were attached, but it was in a lovely quiet suburb of Oxford. To me the house seemed so big with both upstairs and downstairs accommodation, a number of bedrooms, a living room, a large kitchen and a bathroom. And in their back garden they had a large hen coop. It was a tremendous cultural shock to me considering our small house in

Abbeyhill where you literally could not swing a cat and where we had no bathroom.

I can't remember all of the details of our holiday, but on reflection it must have been a tonic to get away from Edinburgh and to be looked after for two weeks and not have time to dwell on our mother's death. I do recall that her death was never mentioned during our time in Oxford, nor was it in Edinburgh by other family members. It was as though people were frightened to mention it for fear of upsetting my brother and I. Relegating my mother's death to the unspoken may well have been a 'Scottish thing' meaning that you have to learn to accept the hand dealt out to you and get on with your life in a stoic way.

I remember on my first morning going down into the hen coop and picking an egg for my breakfast. Whilst there were hen coops in Edinburgh, I had never been in one before and got great satisfaction in choosing a large brown egg which contained thick orange yoke for my breakfast. It was at Oxford that I first tasted fried tomatoes for breakfast; I have had a life-long love of tomatoes ever since.

Bedtime was also different for us as we all had to have a bath each night before bed. Uncle Jimmy would come up to make sure that my brother and I and James were clean and in our pyjamas before going off to bed. Bedtime was a bit of fun as the three of us shared the same bed. As a result I spent a lot of time telling silly boy jokes and breaking wind before eventually getting to sleep.

For me the highlight of the holiday was helping the milkman deliver milk each morning. James must have been in the habit of helping the milkman some mornings and one day we went along to help and I went on to help him each morning. I used to sit beside the milkman as he drove his small electric van, which had a bar across the front of the cabin instead of a driving wheel, whilst the others delivered the milk. I remember the milkman allowing me to drive the milk van with him by my side. I was thrilled.

Uncle Jimmy could be strict at times and was a bit of a 'Jekyll and Hyde' character as he could be easy going one minute and then very serious the next. I always felt that James had a hard time of it as his father was always on his back so to speak. However, Uncle Jimmy was always proud of James and held him in high regard. And whilst Uncle Jimmy could be a hard taskmaster, I always respected him. I don't ever recall him ever raising his voice to me and we did have some laughter-filled times whilst on holiday. In later years, as I grew older, I became more comfortable with him and well remember when he visited my father who was very ill at the time; Uncle Jimmy broke down in tears as he wished my father all the best prior to his returning home to South Africa.

Aunty Minnie was a lovely person and more easy-going. I believe that she was suffering from shingles either before or during our visit to Oxford, as I seem to recall her to be very tired on occasions. There was obviously no after-effect from her illness as she lived in South Africa to the ripe old age of 101years.

My cousin Sheila was older than me and I think at the time had just started a career as a trainee nurse. She was a lovely person and I liked her a lot as amongst other things she had a lovely temperament and always took an interest in my brother and me. It was a tragedy when, a number of years later, she died in South Africa leaving behind a husband and a young son.

I well remember the morning we were to leave Oxford to go back home to Edinburgh. I awoke to the sun shining brightly through the windows. I was the only one in bed as David and James must have gotten up earlier. The radio was playing and I could hear the song very clearly. It was a song sung by the well-known singer of that period called Gracie Fields and the first line of the lyrics went something like this, "Now is the hour when we must bid goodbye, soon you'll be sailing far across the sea". It seemed so appropriate for the occasion and I have always remembered the song. It will always be associated with Oxford for me.

We were accompanied back to London by Uncle Jimmy and settled onto the train for our journey back to Edinburgh. I remember him giving us some pocket money for the journey and Aunty Minnie had made us some sandwiches for the long trip back. The highlight of the return journey for me was having afternoon tea in the dining car. I still remember the starched white tablecloths and unusually shaped sandwiches and fancy small cakes. My memory of what happened was that I kept pestering my brother about wanting to go into the dining car for afternoon tea and somehow I must have found out what it cost and had counted my money and found that I had enough. But, according to my brother many years later, what really happened was that a lady in our compartment, who heard me grumbling, took pity on me and offered to take me in for tea, and I had tea with her and that was how I realised my dream of eating in the dining car.

We arrived at Waverley Station around seven o'clock on Saturday evening and were met by my father who had a smile as long as Leith Walk spread across his face. Mostly because he was glad to see us both, but also because his beloved Hearts had beaten the Glasgow Rangers six-nil at Tynecastle; he was over the moon with joy. I was very disappointed with the result as at that stage of my life, even though I was deemed too young to go to football matches, I used to follow the Rangers through the radio and the newspapers. A particular favourite player of mine was the Rangers goalkeeper, Bobby Brown, who was dropped the following week and, as I recall, never played for the Rangers first team again. I was devastated.

As I grew older, and had more sense, I eventually began supporting the Hearts and spent many happy Saturdays watching them at their beloved Tynecastle and also in other parts of Scotland when they were travelling to play away from home.

Chapter 10

Whilst we were in Oxford it was arranged that Aunty Bella and Aunty Ada would help to clean our house and do our washing on a weekly basis. My father was very close to both of his sisters and we would never have coped after my mother died without their help. I have always been eternally grateful for the way they supported my father and David and I throughout the years until my father died 14 years later. It would have been difficult for them as they had husbands and children to look after, not to mention the travelling back and forth to our house in all kinds of weather.

David, who went to Leith Academy Secondary School after qualifying from Leith Academy Primary School, must have been about 13 years old at this time. He took over the role of message boy in our household and used to get the groceries from the shops on Easter Road and also the weekly groceries from St Cuthbert's on a Saturday. And as David was older, apart from his shopping duties, he was generally responsible for keeping his eye on me and also for taking our washing to Aunty Bella or Aunty Ada by public transport. I was left with not too many responsibilities.

My father took over the role of cook and I must say that his first efforts were hard to stomach. I remember coming home one Sunday afternoon, not long after my mother's death, and sitting down to a plate of beef stew which consisted of half-cooked beef, which was tough to eat, and watery gravy which was almost tasteless. I remember wondering what the future held without my mother and how we would all cope. I suppose being the youngest in the house and not having the experience to help out, I was feeling low and helpless and perhaps a little bit selfish for thinking the way I did.

My father's cooking did improve over the following months but we still consumed a lot of bread rolls with butter, fish suppers, and pies and cream pastries from the local bakery. His most successful meal at this time was his version of stovies and sliced sausage; this consisted of slices of sausage meat, potatoes, plenty of onions and lard all boiled in the same pot. It was guaranteed to fill you up and sky-rocket your cholesterol levels.

I started to take an interest in cooking and began making the Sunday meal when I was about thirteen years of age. I began with tinned chicken noodle soup, boiled chicken and vegetables, and tinned Australian peaches with carnation milk for dessert. I am glad to say that I did improve greatly over the years and believe these early days gave me an introduction to cooking which I never forgot.

As mentioned previously, David had passed his qualifying exam to go from Leith Academy Primary School to Leith Academy Secondary School which I must say was a great feat given the trauma of our mother's illness during his qualifying years. I remember that my father was very pleased as he thought that David would have a better chance of getting a good job when he left school. And although going to Leith Academy may have given David a chance to go to university because of its strong academic stream, this option was never an issue with my father as the main purpose of an education, as he saw it, was to get a good job or trade when you left school. In hindsight, my father was a willing prisoner of the class system and as a working-class person at that time, he saw his role as getting his sons into a job. The opportunity for one of his sons to move from working class to middle class by going to university and working hard would never have crossed his mind. This was a great shame as David had a talent for drawing and would have made a great draftsman or designer. I remember him bringing home his painting of all the Walt Disney characters, which he had painted at school and everyone thought that David showed great promise in art.

41

Because of my age and few responsibilities, I spent a lot of my time with my grandmother and, as I mentioned before, spent my time between my home and hers. In many ways we looked after each other. I had become her message boy and would run all her errands and apart from getting her brandy, these errands were many and varied. They ranged from getting her weekly supply of 'lugs', which I'll describe later, to posting her weekly green Dispatch and pink Saturday Evening News sports papers, which were wrapped around a box of sweets called Edinburgh Rock, to Uncle Jimmy in Oxford. I used to buy the Edinburgh Rock for her from Jackie Challanders sweetie shop on Easter Road, just down from Wilson's fish shop.

Jackie Challanders sweetie shop was a child's ultimate dream as it was stocked from wall to wall with all the sweets and chocolates under the sun. There were pear drops, jap desserts, sherbet lemons, holland toffees, dainty bars, fry's cream and rhubarb rock to name but a few; more than enough to tantalise a young child. The wonderful aroma of the multitude of confectionery has stayed with me all my life and whenever I come across a 'sweetie shop' I will go in hoping to recreate the wonderful smell I first discovered so long ago on Easter Road.

I also used to love to go to Wilson's the fishmonger to see all the fish lying on a marble slab covered in ice. I would stare into the big head and eyes of the different fish; this brings me to the explanation of 'lugs'. A lug is an old Scottish word which translates to the ears of man or animal, but we tended to use it in reference to the side cuttings off the head of the fish. I used to take the parcel of fish off-cuts back to my granny and she would then boil them and give them to Toby, her angry and ballistic cat. The lugs cost about three pence and would last for a few days. The boiling process was quite sickening and the smell of the fish boiling on top of the fire lingered around the small house for hours. The only two in the house that seemed not to care were my granny and Toby who invariably lay in front of the fireplace unusually serene and purring in anticipation. My granny loved her cat and they were great company for each other.

As my grandmother was a great Hibs supporter, I would wait every Saturday evening at the top of Easter Road at around five o'clock for the paper sellers to receive their bundle of papers which had all the football scores and match reports. If I recall correctly, there was always a battle between the Dispatch and the Evening News to deliver and sell the sports news first to the people waiting to find out the results of the day's football.

I loved my time staying with my granny, especially in the winter evenings when we would sit in front of the fire listening to the radio. Sometimes we would hear the wailing of the local tramp, Burnie, who used to shuffle along the centre of Rossie Place singing as best he could in a voice that you could only call mournful. My granny would always give me something for the old man, whether it was a farthing coin or some bread, and ask me to run across the road and give it to him. Burnie was called that name because he had a bright red beard like burning fire. I remember that he always wore a heavy overcoat both in winter and summer and that he was always thankful for whatever he received. Even as a young boy I thought that my granny was great in the way she helped out the old man as she lived only on her government pension and the money my father would give her for helping to look after me.

At my granny's, we would always have a hot cup of cocoa before bed. Then my granny would put out the gas lamp and shuffle off to bed with her candlestick holder burning brightly.
She slept in a very small room, which was called a box room and did not have a proper window although it did have a window of sorts above her bed. It was only about one metre squared and opened out into the stairwell of her tenement. I was much more fortunate as I slept in a big bed in the alcove of the kitchen/living room. I used to love lying there watching the embers of the coal fire light up the room and flickering up the wall whilst the gaslight slowly dimmed before going out.

Saturdays were always fun days for me, as I would go off to the Capital Cinema or the 'Cappi' as all the kids affectionately called it. I would go with friends, or on my own, and tried never to miss it; I loved the cartoons, Tarzan and Roy Rogers, but most of all the serials which always ended on an exciting note and left you anticipating the next week's episode. I used to walk to my granny's from the Cappi which was not far from the bottom of Easter Road and it would only take me 15 minutes or so, and on the way home I would buy two hot pies for our lunch.

During the winter months my granny always made me stovies on a Saturday and she would spoon them on top of the hot pie and I would sit at a table in front of the fire eating contentedly and thinking about the films I had seen that morning. Stovies, as my grandmother made them, were potatoes and onions cut into pieces and cooked slowly in a pan with only a covering of water on the bottom of the pan, a tablespoonful of roast beef dripping and some salt and pepper. They were delicious.

In retrospect my grandmother replaced my mother as in the early days I did find it difficult and strange living in an all male household without my mother. I enjoyed my frequent stays with my granny and in many ways it was a circuit breaker for me; it gave me a chance to recover, and I suppose grieve at my own pace, after the trauma of my mother's death.

In the early days after my mother's death, whenever I went out some woman, never a man, would invariably stop me on Easter Road and asked how I was getting on. Before long her presence would have encouraged another of her acquaintances to gravitate towards us. I became the 'wee soul' who had just lost his mother. I used to hate this 'celebrity status' and would feel like crawling under a rock as they looked down on me shaking their heads in pity. Their questions about, "Who does your washing?" and, "Can your father cook?" bordered on nosiness cloaked in a veneer of interest, but generally people were very supportive and protective, especially people who lived in my street.

It was around this period that I learned to become a very good whistler. I disliked the dark and walking along to my Granny's house on a winter's night would bother me. Her house was in the back of the tenement and you had to walk into a pitch black stairwell, knock on the door and then wait for her to open it. My antidote to this was to whistle, and to whistle loudly, and whenever I was out at night alone and the streets were quiet I would whistle away my fears; as time went by I became a very good whistler.

Chapter 11

After my mother's death I began to hate school and the thought of going there. I remember lying in bed in the early hours of the morning with my stomach churning and dreading the time when I would have to get up and get ready for school. It was at this period that I started to skip school. I would always end up back at my granny's house. I suppose I was suffering from what you would call stress and anxiety, perhaps even depression. Unfortunately it was not a thing people talked about as I guess it was seen as unmanly. Sufferers just had to suffer in silence. It was certainly something that I never discussed or articulated in any way.

At this stage of my life I could easily have gone completely off the rails and gotten in with the wrong crowd, but I believe that my upbringing and an understanding of what was right and what was wrong kept me grounded.

When I escaped from school, it was a friend of my granny, Mrs Ramsey who lived upstairs from her, who always took me back. I can still remember this little woman who was born in the highlands of Scotland, and who must have been at least seventy years old at that time, marching me hand in hand back to school.

During my early years in Edinburgh I began to realise that there was something decent and noble about working-class people. Mrs Ramsey was a prime example of this. Not only did she have to look after a large family of grown up adults who lived with her, but she also made time to prepare a plate from the family Sunday roast dinner and take it down to my granny. She did this for years, as well as helping out when I needed to be taken back to school.

Another example of the decency of the working class was Mr & Mrs Clark who lived opposite Mrs Ramsey and who knew my father and his parents when they were young. Most Sunday mornings, when I was bored and somewhat lonely, I would knock on their door. Invariably Mr Clark would answer in a fashion like this. "Have you no got a home to go to? Aw, come on in". He had a heart of gold although he did not like to show it. We would sit and talk and Mrs Clark would always have a pot of potato soup on the stove. She was the first person to tell me how to make potato soup, her trick was to grate all the vegetables and use mutton flank as her stock base. It was Mr Clark who suggested that I join the Boys' Brigade and who, years later, got me a job as an apprentice brass turner at Lamont's, Corstorphine where he worked as warehouse manager. And it was Mrs Clark who I confided in years later when my father was diagnosed with leukaemia. I can still remember her words, "Aw son, what a shame".

After the collapse of Miss Temper in class and her non-return to school, the wonderful Miss Aitken, possibly because I had fallen behind in my schoolwork due to my mother's illness, took a great interest in me. And apart from trying to help me catch up before the qualifying secondary school exams, she also encouraged me to become involved in singing and the end-of-year school play. She loved singing and used to encourage her pupils to sing solo in the classroom as she did herself. In retrospect, she was a born teacher who cared about all of her pupils, not just the brainy ones. I always loved singing and with Miss Aitkin's encouragement, I joined the school choir. I remember a particular night where we sang in a school competition at the Usher Hall and came fifth.

Because of Miss Aitken my whole approach to school changed and I began to look forward to it again; the years towards the end of primary school were a happy time for me. I remember very clearly Miss Aitken trying to organise for my father to come to watch me in the school end-of-year nativity play where I played one of the wise men. He was working night shift and Miss Aitken went out of her way to arrange for my father to come into the back of the school hall, in his railway uniform, to watch a part of the play before he went off to work. I don't recall now if he did turn up, but I know she tried everything to make it possible for him to do so.

However, despite Miss Aitkin's best efforts, I did not emulate my brother David and qualify for Leith Academy Secondary School, and because of this, I had to enrol at Norton Park Junior Secondary School. I would have been around 12 years of age at this time and whilst I did not dwell on my failure to qualify, in the back of my mind I always felt a little bit badly about the money wasted in sending me to a fee-paying school instead of a state-run one.

Years later, both in Edinburgh and in Australia, I was able to catch up on my education and was awarded a place in an Arts Degree course at Queensland University, which I was unable to take up because of our tight financial situation at the time.

As I became happier at school, I joined in more things. I even tried out for the school rugby team. The selection for the teams was quite demeaning for a young boy, although some would say it was character building. Each Friday afternoon the sports master would read out the names of the team and at the same time throw a team jersey to the chosen players. If you were a reserve player you did not get a jersey but were told to turn up to the game next day, and if you were lucky to get a game, you had to be content to use the soiled jersey of the injured player which you were replacing. And although football was my favourite sport I used to love it, when on the odd occasion, I was chosen to play for the rugby team and I would walk home or sit on the bus carrying the coveted jersey for all to see.

Sadly it was around this time that my granny died. She was found dead at around eight o'clock on a May morning. She was 77 years of age. I remember going around to see her that morning prior to going to school but she did not answer the door. It was the neighbours who called for the police and a local policeman arrived, broke the window in the little box room that served as her bedroom and managed to climb through. He found her dead in bed. It was assumed that she had died some time during the night.

I can't remember going to her funeral, but I do recall the reception at her house after the funeral. There were no outsiders in attendance, only my grandmother's immediate family. I recall that the atmosphere was a little bit tense and crowded. We lunched on the obligatory boiled ham sandwiches and some small cakes from the local bakery in the small kitchen/living room where I had spent so many happy hours with my grandmother.

After lunch my father and I walked home to Alva Place. Another chapter of my life had closed and all I had left were memories of a grandmother who taught me the meaning of loyalty and support; she had supported me, and I her, in our time of need.

Soon after my grandmother's death, David started his apprenticeship as a bookbinder with Peter Nimmo's in Leith. I know my father was very pleased when David was able to get an apprenticeship in the printing industry as it was thought to be a well-paid and respected job.

David's apprenticeship meant that I took over the role of message boy. This suited me fine as it was now my job to buy the occasional cream pastries that we used to eat with our evening meal. In the early stages after my mother's death, we used to buy food from the fish and chip shop on a regular basis, but as we all learned to cook a little bit better we tended to buy less fish suppers and cook more at home.

Living in an all male home had its compensations as I was able to eat more junk food than what was good for me. This probably resulted in increased cholesterol levels in later years, but it was good whilst it lasted.

One of the jobs that I absolutely hated was taking our weekly washing to Aunty Ada or Aunty Bella. We used to put the washing in an old kit bag and I would sit on the Corporation bus holding it and dreading seeing anyone who may have known me. Invariably, if I did see someone who knew me, the first question they would ask as they pointed at the kit bag would be, "What's that?" and, "Where are you going?". This always embarrassed me, as I then had to explain that my mother was dead and that I was taking our washing to my aunties to be cleaned. As a young person I guess I did not want to be different. I just wanted to be like other youngsters as I never subscribed to the 'poor me' syndrome. I saw my situation as one of a bit of bad luck and something that I had to live with. It did not mean that I did not on occasions wonder, "Why me?" There were lots of times that I was incredibly lonely. That was until the time that I started a part-time job as a delivery boy for Gunn's the Grocer after school.

However, it was not all sadness between my mother's death up until I started working at Gunn's. I used to love bonfire night which celebrated Guy Fawkes Night on November the 5th. We would spend weeks, after school and on weekends, calling on houses in our area asking for old furniture or rubbish which we could use as material for the bonfire. Then we would store the rubbish in the back green at Rossie Place. Some of the younger children were given the job of guarding the rubbish; they would call out if children from other streets tried to steal any of our rubbish for their bonfire. I used to love the excitement of the occasion and bonfire night could never come quickly enough for me. I must say that our bonfire in Rossie Place was always a reasonable size, and the fireworks were a kaleidoscope of colour and noise.

I used to love the roman candles and the rockets for their colour, whilst others seemed to enjoy throwing noisy bangers and crackerjacks at the feet of unsuspecting victims. On occasion, if the fire got too big, the fire brigade would be called to extinguish the flames. I remember a window or two cracking from the heat of the bonfire and the fire brigade being called. Bonfire nights were not without risks and I have witnessed children being burned through a combination of misused fireworks and excitement.

Another cause for celebrations in our street was the Coronation of Princess Elizabeth in June 1953. A committee was set up to organise a street party to celebrate this occasion, and I remember my father and I going to our neighbour, Mrs Glasgow's house to watch the coronation on television; she had hired one and people from the street paid to go to her house to watch it. The coronation was televised for the first time to a viewing audience of over 20 million people.

We had a great time cleaning our street from top to bottom and putting up bunting and flags. Most people tidied up their gardens and in some cases even applied a coat of paint where necessary. The party was a great success we had all sorts of games, a bite to eat and all of the children received a coronation mug and a special silver coin to mark the occasion.

Chapter 12

The real difficulty for children in one-parent families, especially those where the father is the surviving parent, is being able to talk about your problems or concerns and sharing the good things that have happened during your day. I have always been brought up not be envious of other people; that envy and jealousy would eat into your personality and eventually make you an unhappy and bitter person, but I have to say that as a child I used to envy my friends as they ran home after school to their mothers for something to eat and to blether about school and their homework and their aspirations.

I especially disliked coming home to a dark and soulless house in winter when my father worked on the back shift. I would have to tidy up the house and get any groceries which were required and then wait for my brother to come home from work. And whilst I would normally do these things without complaint, sometimes, out of sheer frustration, I would occasionally throw my hands in the air, rebel and would go off to the pictures, go out to play or just walk about the streets. The end result of all this would be that my brother would come home from work and he would have to catch up with the house work that I hadn't done leaving him frustrated and angry with me although thankfully it was never for long.

Whilst David and I never discussed our mother's death - we basically just got on with our lives - I am sure that her death affected him very much. He would have been very close to my mother and to lose her at 13 years of age would have been devastating for him. He must also have had a better understanding of her illness and possibly known that she was going to die. On top of that he also had the additional burden of being the oldest child which meant that more was expected of him; he had the responsibility of having to look after me and of doing the household chores until I grew up a little bit. He was four years older than me and by the time I started secondary school, he was commencing his apprenticeship and moving in a different social sphere to me.

I remember on one occasion, just before my 16th birthday, I asked my father for my first suit. My father refused saying that I was too young to have a suit, but David protested to my father saying that I was old enough to get a suit and that I should have one. There was a long argument with my father, and David accused him of being mean. The issue was finally settled when Aunty Ada got involved and she said to my father, "Arthur, the laddie needs a suit" and so it was that I got my first suit.

My father normally listened when Aunty Ada had something to say: they both respected each other. There was a bit of history in their relationship and my Aunty Ada once told me that when she and my father were living at home, he expected his mother to serve him steak for his dinner as he paid more for housekeeping due to his higher earnings. Seemingly, Aunty Ada was not impressed with 'that nonsense' and told my father so in no uncertain terms. It did not affect their relationship however, as they both remained very close.

The matter of 'the suit' did not end there, however as I also wanted some drainpipe trousers which were all the rage. As the name suggests, drainpipe trousers had narrow legs with 16 inch wide bottoms. However my father would not be moved as he said he was not going to have any 'Teddy Boys', the 1950s equivalent of skinheads, in his house and I had to settle for 17inch bottoms.

Grandmother and Grandfather Bews

Grandmother Mackenzie

Grandfather Mackenzie and
cousin James Mackenzie

From L to R: Uncle Alec Bickerton, Father, Mother and
Aunty Doll

Me and my older brother David

My mother and father
before they were married

My mother, David (left) with me
and Prince in Mrs Elder's garden
at 16 Alva Place

My brother David (left) and a
friend with Mrs Elder at
Burntisland

Me and Mr Elder on an afternoon drive

LEITH ACADEMY PRIMARY SCHOOL · · 1952

Me (back row 2nd from the right) in Year 4-5 at
Leith Academy Primary School

Aunty Ada and Uncle
Alec Hood at Rothesay

Front row from L to R: Me, James
Mackenzie & Moira Hood
Middle row from L to R: Sheila
Mackenzie, David Bews & Charlie
Owen
Back row: Ella Owen and Uncle
Jimmy

From R to L:
Uncle Charlie, my
father, Cousin Moira,
Aunty Ada, Aunty Bella
(not sure of the other 3)
and me playing
'goalkeeper'

Mr and Mrs Melrose, Me, Eleanor, Graeme and
Skippy the dog in Mr & Mrs Melrose's backyard

David and Norma's wedding.
From L to R: Norma's parents William & Catherine
Morton, Tom White, David and Norma, Norma's sister
Irene, me, Aunty Doll and my father

An AUEW Burns Supper: 'Cutting the Haggis'
From L to R: Dick Van Hagen (My shop steward at
Lamonts), David Forbes, Bobby Irvine, Ernie Leslie, Bill
McWilliams, someone I can't recall, John Boyd, Gavin
Laird, Bobby Irvine and Jack Keddie

Photograph from The Scotsman Publications Limited

Me presenting the cheque for the school bus to
Reverend Colin Anderson with Betty Morris

Photograph by Campbell Harper Studios Ltd

Gift from shop floor

Worker participation in the realms of community service took on a new significance in Pilton when the management committee of the district's Youth Retreat at Ratho received a gift of more than £400 from employees of Ferranti's engineering works at Crewe Toll, Edinburgh.

The money, which has been raised by a variety of projects at the factory, is being used to help to meet the cost of a new mini-bus which has just been acquired by the Retreat.

The workers' interest in the Retreat's drive to obtain a vehicle began in January, after Councillor Charles R. Stuart, Labour representative for the St Giles' Ward and chairman of the education committee, contacted Mr Alan Bews, convener of shop stewards at Ferranti's, on hearing of the need for a mini-bus.

After a meeting, the representatives of the eight unions at the factory agreed to organise a fund-raising programme, and the Ferranti Employees' Pilton Retreat Fund was set up, with Mr Bews as chairman.

Then the committee set to work. A factory collection was followed up by a dance, and later a folk concert. The effort was rounded off by an Easter Fair in the Old Kirk's hall at Pennywell Road, and a raffle.

TABLET

The takings were eventually boosted to £407.78 with a donation of £46.18 from one of the factory women employees, who sold home-made tablet and toffee outside the works.

When Mr Bews and a fund-raising committee colleague, Miss Betty Morris, called at the Old Kirk to

FACTORY WORKERS RAISE £400 FOR YOUTH BUS

hand over the cheque to the Rev. Colin Anderson, they were shown the mini-bus.

The vehicle cost £1500, of which £700 was provided by a grant from the corporation's education committee, so the Ferranti gift will meet about half the remainder.

Mr Bews said : " We had hoped to raise a bit more, but when we reached the £400 mark we realised that this was about as far as we could go."

The Rev. Colin Anderson, minister of the Old Kirk and a member of the Retreat's management committee, added : " I am impressed again as I have been in the past by the willingness of the Ferranti employees to exercise themselves and promote this idea for the benefit of the people who live beside the place where they work.

Mr Anderson, the factory's chaplain, added : " They deserve credit for something which went well beyond the requirement of their union membership. It cements the relationship between the workpeople of Ferranti's and the residents of the community, like the Old Kirk, and their community activities."

PICTURE SHOWS: The Rev. Colin Anderson (right), minister of the Old Kirk, Pennywell Road, " acting treasurer " as Mr Alan Bews (left) and Miss Betty Morris (second right), hand over the cheque. With them are Mr Victor Lindsay (second left), the Retreat committee's organising secretary, and Pete Holberton, warden at Ratho. Behind them is the mini-bus.

Newspaper article from the, *Evening News, Edinburgh*

15·4·72·

03·30·

Court of Session, Scotland.

PETITION

of

FERRANTI LIMITED   PETITIONERS

against

A. Bews and Others.   RESPONDENTS

19**7**2

First page of Interim Interdict received
during the machine tool department
dispute

Above: District Committee members and guests at the
opening of new Union premises on Morrison Street

Below: Ferranti Thistle U21 Juvenile Football Team the
winners of the Bob Tait trophy

Photograph by Campbell Harper Studios Ltd

Above: Union friends at my farewell presentation.
From L to R: Eric Mason (Tollcross branch secretary), George
Lyall (shop steward), Me, Dougie Rooney (newly-elected
convener, Ferranti), Les Stirling (Works Council, Ferranti) and
Jim McNicol (Musselburgh branch secretary)

Photograph by Robb and Campbell Harper Limited

Back row from L to R: Uncle Alec Bickerton, Aunty
Doll, Cousin Maureen, Great Aunt Elizabeth (from
Findhorn) and David.
Front row from L to R: Cousin Joan, me and Norma

Our wedding
day
October30th,
1971

David and I at Waverley
Station, Edinburgh just prior
to leaving for Australia

From Left: Aunty Bella,
Aunty Minnie & Aunty Ada

Chapter 13

My first day at Norton Park was an eye-opener to me. I walked to school, as it was only ten minutes from my house. The school looked out onto Easter Road Park, the home pitch of the Hibs. The first thing that I noticed as I walked down Easter Road and into Bothwell Street, was the different types of clothes worn by the pupils as there was no uniform regulation. There were also a number of people smoking and I could hear a lot of swearing as I passed other students on my way to school. I stood in line with other first year students. I was anxious and wondered how I was going to handle the change from the fee-paying, privileged and disciplined Leith Academy to this new environment. I was allocated into class B4, which was lower than I expected; B6 was the lowest class in the year.

The school building was old and the school annex, which housed all the technical classes such as metalwork, carpentry, technical drawing and arts, was a five-minute walk away from the main school. The annex was a long and narrow old brick building and inside was a long windowless corridor where you would line up in your class group at the door of your classroom. I recall that in the summer the corridor was always hot, and in the winter it was always cold and the noise was always deafening.

School dinners were provided at a small cost and it was a shock to me to find out that dinners were served in classrooms and that you sat at your desk to eat your meal. Needless to say, the first class of the afternoon would be greeted by the wonderful leftover smell of school dinners. In contrast, dinners at Leith Academy Primary School were served in the school dining room; in clean and pleasant surroundings. From my viewpoint, the contrast between the schools could not have been more striking. I began to realise why my mother wanted to give my brother and I every opportunity in education by sending us to a fee-paying school.

Whilst most of the pupils were reasonable, there were a number of them from disadvantaged backgrounds who caused a lot of heartache to other pupils with their bullying and violent dispositions. As a result of their dislike for authority, classes could be thrown into turmoil by their antics. If my recollection is correct, the teachers tried their best which must have been difficult given the obstacles. Some of the pupils there were not interested, and therefore disruptive. They saw Norton Park as a means to an end, as at 15 years of age they would leave school and look for a job with or without their Junior Leaving Certificate.

I remember one carpentry teacher, a decent person who was well respected by the class but who seemed to suffer from stress; at the beginning of each class he would have the class stand quietly at our benches as he sat with his hand over his eyes for two or three minutes trying to relax before the class started. Another teacher, one who taught English, spent most of the period reading western novels to the class. His favourite, and ours, was the classic western, *Shane*, which later became a big film success. Needless to say there were never any problems in his class.

I never ever was able to understand Technical Drawing or read drawings very well as our technical drawing teacher was an elderly man who lost his temper with little provocation. He seemed to have no self-control and would scream and hit those students who drew badly or who did not understand what they were being taught. If I recall correctly, he later had a nervous breakdown, but his illness was no help to me as he had totally put me off the subject by that stage.

Because of the circumstances of my earlier life I had developed a streetwise persona which was to become useful to me at my new school. My father was always counselling me to weigh people up, and if I thought they were not decent, then to stay clear of them. He was forever giving me money to go to the cinema when he worked the back shift. I assume he felt I would be safer in the cinema with less chance of getting bored or getting into mischief.

During my three years at Norton Park, I went through the motion of attending school regularly and on time. Eventually, after a year or so, I began to lose any interest I had in school as I was doing very badly at maths and most of the technical subjects, and I was barely passing in the others. There were two reasons for this: firstly, I was under no scrutiny at home as my father never discussed homework and as long as I attended school he was satisfied. In fairness to my father, I believe he knew that I was struggling and that I did not like school, but he did not want to pressure me in any way because of our difficult home life.

The second reason was that through my friendship with Mr and Mrs Clark's son, Robert, I got a job as a grocery delivery boy at Gunn's the grocer, which was at the end of Rossie Place and almost opposite my grandmother's old house. I would report to Gunn's at three-thirty pm Tuesday, Thursday and Friday and work until six pm, and on a Saturday I would work from eight-thirty am until five pm. This made my week very full, as I also had to buy our groceries, take our washing to be cleaned and help out at home, as well as rush home after school dinner to buy some lunch for my father when he worked night shift, and then get back to school in time for the afternoon class. Because of all this, school became something to be endured rather than enjoyed and I could not wait for the bell to ring at the end of daily lessons.

I was paid 17 shillings and sixpence a week by Gunn's, which I gave to my father for board but I kept all the tips which were very generous, especially during Christmas and New Year. I used to make about 15 shillings to a pound in tips during normal weeks, but at Christmas and New Year I could make up to five pounds per week.

I used to deliver the groceries on a bicycle which had a cage attached to the front in which I would place the grocery box and then cycle off to the customer's address which could be a mile or two from the shop. In some respects it was a tough job as the weather could be really difficult, especially in the winter with cold winds, sleet and snow, rain or fog, and after four pm darkness would set in. It was also very difficult cycling uphill as was the case if you delivered groceries to one of the Foreign Embassies on Royal Terrace. However there was always the excitement of cycling downhill on the way back. We delivered to most of the Embassies but as deliveries go it was not a good run as it was a steep hill and there were never any tips.

As Gunn's was a licensed grocer, at an early age I got to know the different alcoholic drinks that were available. The shop was very well patronised and sold a wide range of cold meats, cheeses, butter and biscuits and in many ways was similar to today's delicatessen. It was an age when people queued up for their groceries and butter was cut to weight from a large block that sat on a marble slab. Mr Gunn was like a character from a Dickens novel; he sat on a high stool at his desk entering all the business transactions into his ledger with a pen and ink. He also organised all the wages for the staff. He was a quiet man who did not serve behind the counter. Jimmy Wilson was in charge of the staff that worked behind the counter. He generally ran the shop with Mr Gunn. Some time later he was to buy part of the business and the shop was to become known as Gunn & Wilson.

There were only two delivery boys, Robert Clark and myself, and when he left a few months after I started I became the longest serving grocery delivery boy. By that stage I had got to know all the different customers, especially those who tipped well. When we were not delivering groceries, we worked downstairs cleaning the cellar where all the alcohol and soft drinks were stored, and where they cured the boiled hams that sold in the shop. I was always fascinated by the way the grocer skinned the outside of the ham with his fingers leaving a thick covering of fat around the boiled ham, or gammon as it was also known. I persuaded one of the grocers to show me how it was done and

74

before long I was given the job of skinning the hams. I used to delight taking the hams upstairs to the shop and placing them on the cold meat shelving in the front window.

Mrs White, who was the head lady shop assistant, and whose husband used to play for the Hearts football team, was very good to me and always kept the off-cuts from the meat slicer for me and I would take them home at the end of the day. Because of the exercise I got from delivering the groceries I was very fit and could eat as much as I liked without putting on weight. I could also eat copious amounts of broken biscuits and any meats and cheeses that were available. In many ways it was a dream job for a young teenager.

When Pepsi Cola came on the market, the bottles were stored in the cellar and it was a terrible temptation for me, my fellow delivery boy and the apprentice grocer as there had been a very good advertising campaign extolling its virtues. Eventually we all succumbed to the temptation and would allow ourselves an occasional bottle. After drinking them we would break the bottles and put any stock shortages down to breakage. This was my one and only slide into crime and I always felt guilty about it. However, the Pepsi was great, and I am sure that the occasional soft drink taken by the delivery boy was unofficially expected.

I really loved working at Gunn's as it was a circuit breaker for me from school, and I felt that I was contributing something worthwhile and that I was good at what I did. I also felt more confident about myself, made some new friends and gained respect from others during my three years there.

During this period I also joined the Boys' Brigade. Mr and Mrs Clark and their son Robert, who worked with me at Gunn's, suggested that I join. His brother John, who was only in his early twenties, was an officer with them. John Clark was a lovely person, and was well liked by the boys in the brigade as he was much younger than the other officers. He was also a very good piper and taught the pipes to those boys who were interested. I went to a number of his classes but could never master the chanter, which you practiced the pipe tunes on. You also needed to learn how to read music, which I found difficult, but I did manage to get into the Boys' Brigade band as a big drummer. This only required me to beat in tune to the music, which I was able to do. The big drum was a cumbersome instrument especially when playing and marching in a procession. On windy days I could almost be blown off my feet as the force of the wind pulled at the drum.

Our brigade was the 45th Boys' Brigade Unit and was part of the London Road Church. We met each Friday and would spend some time marching and then we would play some sport -mostly five-a-side football. Prior to marching, our uniforms would be inspected and we would be given points for their tidiness. I remember a marching competition which we had hoped to win. Towards the end of the march, as we were marching off the parade ground, my hat began to slip down over my face. I pushed it back onto my head and continued to march. This was a cardinal sin in the eyes of the judges as I should have let my hat fall to the ground without touching it. Because of this, we were deducted points for my indiscretion and did not win the competition. This was akin to a goalkeeper dropping the ball over his goal line in a cup final, in the ninetieth minute, when the score is nil-nil; as a result I was not the most popular person in the brigade at that time.

Each year we had a two-week long camp, which was a great experience. We lived under canvas tents and cooked all our own meals. I remember one year, my brother David and his fiancée Norma Morton came to visit me on parent's day. They took me into Dunbar for a Knickerbocker Glory which was a delicious ice cream treat.

Each Sunday morning we had to attend Bible Class where our captain, Mr Hobson, and some of the other officers would take the service. And afterwards some of us would go to Harry's Café, the local Italian ice cream shop, for a coca-cola or an ice cream drink. There we would discuss things such as whether the Hearts were a better football team than the Hibs and whether Cliff Richards was a better singer that Elvis Presley who at that time was the great pop hero amongst Scottish teenagers.

During the week there were pipe-band classes, swimming classes at Abbeyhill Baths and, in the summer, cricket games which Mr Hobson used to delight in taking because of his love of the game. I felt, probably for the first time, that I began to belong to something else other than my family. It was a good feeling that other people, namely the officers, would take so much time in looking after our interests and taking care of us in this stage of our journey through life. If anyone missed a bible class or a Friday evening meeting, one of the officers would invariably turn up at that person's house to enquire if there were any problems. Our Brigade was a mixture of tough kids, good football players and potential future leaders but what we were all taught for sure was the difference between what was right and what was wrong, and that people should be treated fairly and with dignity. Whether we all heeded our training would remain to be seen, but the Boys' Brigade certainly provided a great social service in trying to guide young boys along a safe path into manhood.

One of the older boys from our brigade, Adam Smith who was a lance corporal, was savagely beaten in the Queen's Park trying to help a smaller boy who was being bullied by a group of young men. He received a broken nose and both his eyes were closed by the force of a head butt to his face. The perpetrators were a group of toughs who lived on East Thomas Street which was a street off Easter Road and was not far from where I lived. And although the majority of the people who lived in East Thomas Street were decent and hard-working, the street got a bad name because of the anti-social behaviour of a few thugs and bullies who lived there. For me it was a no-go area and I tended to stay clear of it if I could. But ironically, when I worked at Gunn's, I had to deliver groceries there on a number of occasions and I was always tipped rather generously by the customers.

77

At the first bible class after the assault, we were advised by Mr Hobson about Adam's injuries and that he had decided, along with another officer, to go to see those responsible and talk to them about their reasons for the vicious assault. We were all shocked that he would even consider such a thing as we were all more street-wise than him, or so we thought. But we knew that he would end up similar to Adam Smith if he went anywhere near East Thomas Street, so we all pleaded with him not to go there and to leave it to the police. Eventually, one of the perpetrators of the attack was given some time in jail for the assault. I am not sure if Mr Hobson ever did make a trip to East Thomas Street to meet those responsible, but if he did it would have stretched his very strong Christian beliefs.

Chapter 14

At the age of 15, I left school to take up an apprenticeship as a brass turner with James H Lamont at their Gylemuir Works in Corstorphine. I left school on Friday January 31st, 1957 and started work the following Monday. I left school with no leaving certificate and shudder to think what would have become of me if Mr Clark had not found me a job at Lamont's where he was warehouse manager. Apart from school I had enjoyed my last three years; I liked working at Gunn's and being a part of the Boys' Brigade. I had gotten used to life at home, organising and getting the groceries and taking the clothes to be washed. And although this did not stop when I started work, my brother shared some of the load until he left home a year or so later to get married to Norma.

On my first day of work I got up at around six am to get ready. I had bought a pair of bib and brace overalls, a pair of work boots and a six-inch rule. As it was February it was very cold and dark. After a quick breakfast I ran up the road to Montrose Terrace to get the Number 26 bus to Corstorphine. From the bus stop at Corstorphine, it took only a few minutes to walk to Lamont's to start my first day's work at 8am. I remember very clearly standing outside the foreman's office on my first morning. My only instruction from Mr Clark was to turn up on time and stand outside the foreman's office and that I would be attended to eventually. There had been no interviews or any formal offer of work other than being told by Mr Clark that I would start as a pre-apprentice and, that if I worked hard, I would be given an apprenticeship as a brass turner on my 16th birthday. I would then serve a five year apprenticeship and become a tradesman by 21 years of age.

And so I waited. Eventually the head foreman, Mr Tammy Brown, at work his name was pronounced Broon, appeared and took me off to the cloakroom to hang up my jacket. He then escorted me on a short trip around the workshop where I was to work. Mr Brown was similar to most head foremen at that time; to denote his status he wore a brown dustcoat over his suit and dress shoes. He smoked a pipe and spoke quite fast yet rather softly. The thing I remember most about Tammy Brown was his habit of standing in the middle of the workshop at starting time and at five minutes before finishing time to catch people out who came in late for work or tried to leave early. In the morning the other foremen would join him for a smoke and blether but they were never there to join him before finishing time. The cynics all joked that it was because they had all knocked off early themselves.

I was introduced to the pre-apprentice who I was replacing; he was starting his apprenticeship the following week. I don't now recall his name but he was a decent sort of character whose job it was to show me my duties. The core part of my job was to get the food for the department at morning break and at lunchtime. I was also expected to help the tradesmen clean their lathes on a Friday afternoon and load the swarf bags full of machine cuttings onto the trolleys. This could be quite hazardous at times as at the beginning I was forever cutting my fingers on the machine cuttings. My other jobs were running errands for the foreman or for the other tradesmen.

Lamont's was a medium-sized company with about 300 employees. It had three machine shops, a pattern-making shop, a foundry, a toolmaker shop, a warehouse and dispatch section, a small first aid room with a first aid lady, and a canteen where lunch was served. There were a number of apprentices and female workers who worked on the lathes beside the tradesmen who were time-served brass turners or brass finishers. There were also semi-skilled workers and labourers who operated the stamping machines, worked in the machine shops, foundry or in warehouse and dispatch.

My first few days were traumatic. Not knowing anyone, I found it difficult the first day and at morning break I hid in the toilets as I

80

felt that I stood out and everyone was looking at me. I still found it exciting and I enjoyed the atmosphere, however it was difficult getting used to the noise in the machine shop. When I was not doing my core jobs, I would be given some simple work to do on the flywheel press or de-burring machine. These jobs could be very boring and I used to look forward to when it was time to get the orders for morning break or lunch. To find out what food everyone wanted for their breaks I had to go to each machine and take people's orders. On my first day, as I went to each person, they would ask me my name and which football team I supported. Part of the reason people asked what team you supported was that they liked to know what religion you were. If you replied the Hearts or the Rangers it would be assumed that you were probably Protestant and if you said the Hibs or Celtic you were more likely to be Catholic. As it turned out, most of the football supporters at Lamont's supported the Hearts, which meant that I at least had something in common with them. When I finished taking the orders, I would then go down to the canteen and work out how many biscuits, sandwiches and packets of crisps were required, tally up the cost and then make sure that I had the correct change when I returned with the food in time for the morning or lunch break.

It was at the canteen that I first met the other pre-apprentices who were there organising their orders. The lady who was in charge of the canteen was called Edna and she was a real tough nut although on occasions she did show a soft spot. There is a saying in Scotland that the women, who pushed themselves in first at the washhouse on washing day to the disadvantage of the other women, were called the 'bully of the washhouse' and Edna certainly deserved that mantle. If you were not organised with your order she would lambaste you mercilessly, and you would take your life in your hands if you criticised her cooking. She did keep a very clean kitchen but unfortunately all the food tasted the same to me - even the chips - not that I would ever have told her that. I can still remember some of the food people ordered. Cheese flavoured crisps, cheese sandwiches and chocolate wheaten biscuits seemed to be the staple diet for some people, although quite a few people brought their own food for morning break and had a cooked dinner in the canteen at lunch time.

During the first few months I got to know people better and I began to like each day as it was usually different to the last. I was learning more about my job and also about the people I worked with. I did find it difficult getting up in the morning especially in the winter when it was cold and wet. It was no problem when my father was working nightshift as he warmed up the house and brought in hot rolls for breakfast, but when it was left up to me to get up when he worked other shifts, I struggled to be on time for the bus and for work.

Most of my workmates were good to get along with and treated me well but, as in life, there were others who liked to take advantage of the new boy; they tended to gang together to make jokes at your expense. I remember one day I was asked by a young tradesman to go to the warehouse and get a long stand. When I got there I told the warehouseman what I had come to collect, he told me to stand at his desk and he would see what he could do. After a while the warehouse manager came out and told me that there was no such thing as a long stand and that the boys were only having a bit of fun. I took this in good spirit as boys at school had warned me that these sort of things happened during your first few weeks at work. A second attempt to embarrass me was to move my jacket from its peg in the cloakroom and hide it under someone else's jacket in another part of the cloakroom. This meant that I had to wait until everyone else had left before I could find my jacket and as a result I would miss my bus. Whilst I had a good idea who was behind the so-called joke, I could only grin and bear it. I put it down to experience and tried never to show that their bullying upset me.

In all, I never really had too many more problems and, with help from other pre-apprentices and some of the older tradesmen who took me under their wing, I slowly became wiser to the antics of the pranksters.

Chapter 15

One of the first friendships that I made at work was with Willie Melrose who was the pre-apprentice in one of the other machine shops. We got to know each other at the canteen as we organised our orders. During the following years, I became great friends with Willie. I was best man at his wedding and a few years later he was best man at mine. I would spend a lot of time at his house on weekends when we started to go to dances at Queensferry and I got to know his parents and brother and sister very well. Mr and Mrs Melrose were lovely people, especially Mrs Melrose who could not do enough for me; she used to serve a wonderful breakfast of bacon and eggs at her home in Clermiston which was only ten minutes from Lamont's.

When I reached the age of sixteen, I started to serve my time as an apprentice brass turner and was given a small capstan lathe to operate, and each day the foreman would come around to ask how many parts I had machined the previous day. The machine was set up by a machine setter who taught me how to operate it. The idea was that I would eventually be able to set the machine up by myself, but that the machine setter could help me if I broke some of the tooling used on the machine.

The first machine setter I was allocated to was Charlie Waters who lived with his wife and son beside the Hearts football ground on Gorgie Road. He was a decent man and we kept in touch up until I left for Australia many years later. A few months after I started work under Charlie, I brought him a cutting tool to be repaired. It was the sixth one I had broken and Charlie said to me in an exasperated but not too serious manner, "If you break another tool, just go home". I was so upset about continually breaking the tools that I began to feel useless and that I would never be able to do the job properly. I was full of self doubt and I took Charlie literally and left the premises. I began to walk home. I don't think I realised what I had done by leaving work without telling anyone, and as I walked away from the building, I was so confused and upset that instead of getting the bus home I started a two hour walk home instead. As I walked along Corstorphine Road towards Haymarket my mood changed from elation that I would never have to go back to Lamont's, to despair as I began to realise what I had done. I walked from Haymarket to the West End and then along Princes Street and I began to imagine what would be happening at Lamont's when they found that I was not on site. As I rounded Calton Hill and went down Montrose Terrace to Abbeyhill I began to wonder what I was going to tell my father who would be home in bed after working the night shift.

When I arrived home my father woke up and asked if I was not well as I had come home early. When I told him the story he was dumbstruck and wanted to know if there were any other reasons that I had left work without telling anyone. He asked if I was being bullied or if I had been in a fight. Was there any other reason that I was so upset as to leave work unannounced? When I told him no, that I just felt so bad and useless about breaking the tools, he said that although it would be difficult for me I would need to go back to work the next day, give them my explanation, and accept any consequences of my actions. He said that in life you have got to face up to adversity, and that if I did not go back to work, the likelihood would be that when I was faced with other problems in life I would walk away without confronting them. Later that day, my father received a hand delivered letter from Mr West, the Works Manager, telling him that I had left work without telling anyone and that as the welfare of their apprentices was important to them they hoped that I had returned home. The letter also said that they looked forward to seeing me at work at eight o'clock the next day.

Later that day I went along the road to see Mr Clark and explain to him what happened and the first words he said to me were, "Why did you run away you silly bugger?. Do you think that you are the only person that has ever broken a few !!!!!!!! cutting tools?".

85

The next morning I reported for work as usual and everyone was very supportive. I apologised to Charlie Waters who I knew would have been worried as I had been told that Mr West had grilled him as to why I had left work without telling anyone. Later that day, I was sent to Mr West's office and he told me in a very decent way that I was never to leave the site without speaking to my foreman again, and that breaking tools was not a hanging offence and with a smile he said, "Well not for six broken tools anyway".

Life between sixteen and eighteen years of age was all about football and work, and work and football. At work most of the apprentices played for juvenile football teams, some of whom were very good players. Willie Melrose was an excellent player and another two of the apprentices played trial games for the Hearts. I managed to get into one of the least successful teams in the Under 17 Juvenile Division called the Edinburgh Rangers; I played left back. I was only an average player. I recall one Saturday afternoon playing Edinburgh Athletic whose players were mostly talented and earmarked to play for senior teams such as the Hearts or Rangers. That afternoon, a player called Willie Henderson was playing right wing. He was loaned out to Edinburgh Athletic by the Glasgow Rangers and was to eventually become one of the great Glasgow Rangers players and a successful Scottish Internationalist. I was playing left back that day and played directly opposite him. I had a nightmare afternoon trying to contain him. He scored a few goals and, needless to say, I was the butt of a few jokes the following Monday when I returned to work.

I would be the first to admit that my brother David was a much better player than me. It caused a bit of excitement in our house one night when a committee member from a local team came to the house to persuade David to sign up for them. I think my father was quite proud to think that a team wanted to sign him up and put themselves out by coming to our house for his signature. Years later, when David visited my family in Australia, I used to joke with him that whenever I used to go to watch him play he was always sitting on the bench hoping to get a game although that was later in his life when injuries and old age were slowing him down.

I remember at work how one of the apprentices was the victim of a practical joke. After bragging about how well he played at the weekend one of the tradesmen, Big Slim, went up to him and said that he had just received a call from the top juvenile side, Tynecastle Athletic, saying that they had watched him play at the weekend and that they wanted him to report for training the following Wednesday evening. Big Slim then gave him a note that he had mischievously written stating the time and venue of the training session. The apprentice was over the moon. Whether the apprentice ever reported for training or not, it certainly stopped him from bragging about his football skills. After that prank, Monday mornings were much quieter.

One of the most disliked practices, which would now be seen as an offence to the individual, was the initiation ceremony which most apprentices had to endure when they completed their apprenticeship. How prevalent this ceremony was in other companies I don't know, but it was certainly alive and kicking at Lamont's. What would happen was that the victim would be captured by young tradesmen, who had recently been victims themselves, and dragged into either the toilet area or the cloakroom where their trousers would be pulled down and machine grease would be applied to their private parts. This practice was one we nearly all had to endure. Some fought and kicked to stop the process but were mostly overpowered. Whilst others, who were more concerned about getting their clothes covered in grease, were more compliant.

During my time at Lamont's Aunty Bella started to do our washing. Aunty Bella lived at Corstorphine, just down the road from Lamont's, so I would have to get up even earlier in the morning to take the washing to her and then to proceed on to work. I would then pick up the washing after work and stay for a wonderful dinner, blether and a bath. Aunty Bella who was a lovely placid person worked part-time for her brother, Uncle Don, who owned his own bakery; there was never a shortage of the occasional broken cake or pie at her place.

Chapter 16

My brother David got married to Norma when I was almost eighteen years of age. I remember going out with him to his stag party two weeks before his wedding. I was excited about this as I was still under-age and should not have been served any alcohol. We met his mates at Mac's Bar on Easter Road just down from Crolla's ice cream shop, which served the best ice cream in Edinburgh, and the pork butcher, which was famous for its red, black and white puddings. I did not have any problems getting served at the bars as I was quite solid and looked as if I was eighteen. We spent a few hours at Mac's Bar and then moved on to a pub at Fountain Bridge before we went off to the Palais de Dance.

I was totally excited about the whole evening and enjoyed the atmosphere of the pubs and also the dancing as it was the first time I had ever been to the Palais. I remember losing track of everyone at the dance and walking home alone. I arrived just before David. We had a great evening.

David and Norma's wedding was held on June 4th, 1960. We all had a great time and I remember it was a very warm and sunny day. Years later, after the birth of their daughters Elizabeth and Sandra, David and Norma moved from their home in Montgomery Street to a new house at Loanhead approximately 20 kilometres outside of Edinburgh. It seemed quite far away at that time.

Not very long after the wedding, I had an accident at work. Whilst machining a part on my lathe, my hand accidentally strayed towards the chuck - the machine part that held the component I was machining - and as the machine stopped, the first joint of my right middle finger was caught between the chuck and the cross slide of the machine. Initially I heard a crunch and then I felt coldness around the top joint of my finger. I remember walking to the female machinist who worked on the machine next to mine and showing her my damaged finger. She called one of the men who worked the stamping machine near her over and he took me to the first aid room where an overenthusiastic nurse threw her hands in the air and shouted out, "Hospital case!". With a heavily bandaged finger I stood waiting outside the first aid room for the company truck to come to take me to the Royal Infirmary. I remember being helped up into the cabin of the truck and being driven off. I still did not feel any great pain. I assume that I would have been in some sort of shock. At the hospital, as two male nurses took me to a ward, I passed our next-door neighbour Mr Elder who was at the hospital for an examination. I shouted to him, "Hello Mr Elder, I have cut the tip of my finger off". I don't know who was more surprised, me or him. At the ward, a doctor advised me that I would have to be admitted as they would need to operate to try to save the finger joint. The nurses then took me to the ward bathroom and helped me take off my clothes then they literally dumped me into a very large bath where they both proceeded to wash me. Moments after that, when I was in my hospital bed I was given a Valium injection which put me on cloud nine whilst I waited to be taken to the operating theatre. Unbeknown to me, the hospital authorities had asked the police to contact my father to get his permission to operate and my father duly arrived at my bedside looking very concerned. I told him through my Valium-induced haze that he was not to worry as it was only a finger tip and it could have been worse. The operation was a success and I only lost the tip of my finger, but I did however become another statistic in workplace injuries.

When I returned to work, our shop steward Dick Van Hagen, who was affectionately known as 'Old Dick' and who coincidentally worked as an apprentice with my grandfather at a company called Laidlaw's, gave me a form to complete in order to claim compensation for my accident. I told Dick that I didn't know how I could make a claim, as I was possibly to blame for the accident. Dick remarked, "Son, no one is 100% to blame for an industrial accident". And so I made a claim and I ended up going to Glasgow by train to meet with the union solicitor. I eventually received 45 Pounds for the loss of the tip of my finger. This equated to approximately 15 weeks wages at that time.

Chapter 17

It was around this period of my life that my father became ill. He would have been around 51 years of age at the time. Initially he started suffering from heavy colds, especially in the chest, which were accompanied by very bad coughs and whatever the doctor prescribed had almost no effect. Then, over a period, he developed an itchy rash all over his body. I spent weeks rubbing ointment all over him even though this too had little effect. Then he became extremely tired, to the point that he did not have the strength to shave in the morning. All this took place over many months until he was eventually hospitalised for some extensive tests and blood transfusions.

After some very unpleasant intrusive tests a young doctor told me that my father had Myeloid Leukaemia and that his prognosis was not good. All he would say was that the very best we could hope for was a maximum of five or six more years of life. The doctor also said that my father's quality of life would not be good as his system would break down progressively. And thus began a roller-coaster life of serious illness, remissions, long periods off work, and short periods at work. I could only look on in admiration at the fighting spirit and will to live that my father displayed during the almost six years which he battled his illness.

I remember two union officials sitting by his bedside at home telling him that if he resigned from work he could get a small payout, which I am sure would have been useful. My father declined their help saying that if he resigned from work it would be the beginning of the end for him as a man needs a purpose in life and working on the railway was his. I suppose it gave him a reason to live and a feeling of belonging.

My father never talked about his illness. He knew that it was terminal but he never ever mentioned that to me and I never let on that I knew how ill he was. Throughout the years of his illness he never complained and he never had an attitude of 'why me?' The nearest he got to mentioning it was one Saturday night as we were leaving to go up to the Artisan Bar. Out of the blue he said to me, "One day all this will be over and you will settle down and get married". It was the one and only time he alluded to his illness. It was as if he was apologising for holding me back as I spent most of my time looking after him.

He loved the Artisan Bar and his Saturday night with his friends Tommy Cannon and Alex Whitehead. They always met at eight-thirty pm and drank until closing time at ten. During the early stages of his illness, I would make my way back to the Artisan before closing time to take him home and, as his illness progressed, I would take him up to the Artisan and stay with him and become part of the group. One of the side effects of his illness was that the steroid drugs and iron tablets made him extremely hungry so, after closing time, we would go up to the local fish and chip shop and buy double fish and pie suppers; there may have been some excuse for my father having double servings, but there was no excuse for me. Still, I loved it.

At one stage, my father was sent to the Marie Curie Cancer and Convalescent Hospital at Cooper in Fife. This meant that we all had to organise visiting times, as it was an hour or two travel time there from Edinburgh. The hospital was built high on the hills above Cooper. It was a wonderful spot for a hospital and an excellent place for a break for those who were sick. One day when I was visiting, I found my father and Uncle Alec in the billiard room playing snooker. I was amazed how good they both were and when I commented on their skills my father jokingly said that it was an example of a misspent youth. Actually, young men of my father's generation were good at billiards and snooker as many of them spent a lot of time during their youth in billiard halls because of unemployment.

My father's death was as quick as it was unexpected. It happened on a cold clear winter's day. I was sitting in his bedroom talking to him about the old lady above us who had died and of how the police were in the process of having her body removed; seemingly they had found her dead, surrounded by bundles of old newspapers that were infested with mice. Suddenly my father clutched the right side of his stomach and gasped. After a few deep breaths he said," Well, that's it then." and laid his head back onto his pillow in some discomfort. These were his last words as he dropped into semi-consciousness. I contacted our doctor, Dr Alexander, who had supported my father during the period of his illness and when he came he gave my father an injection. As he left he said that he would return in the morning but that he did not expect my father to last very long.

I remember the following morning I had put on a large fire as it was cold. Dr Alexander and I were standing in front of the fire as he explained that he had organised for an ambulance to take my father to hospital. Suddenly a mouse ran across the carpet and the doctor exclaimed, "There's a wee moose!" It must have escaped from the house above and, by its actions, it helped bring a bit of laughter into a sad day. I followed the ambulance to the hospital and stayed with my father until he was taken into a ward where they tried to prolong his life, but he had fought his last battle with his illness and was tired out. My father died on the morning of December 19th,1965.

Now because I had been in similar positions before, when against the odds my father had recovered, I had not alerted the other family members that he had relapsed again. But this time, when I went with Uncle Alex to David's work to tell him the sad news, it was very real.

After the funeral, all the men went up to the Artisan Bar for one last drink to my father which was appropriate given that he had spent many happy hours there over the years.

Chapter 18

It had been during the early stages of my father's illness that I became interested in my trade union, the Amalgamated Engineering Union (AEU). My interest started because of the way the union had looked after me when I had damaged my finger. I remember that even as a youngster I thought it was great that an organisation could look after an individual and put forward a legal case for compensation on their behalf. It gave me a good feeling that an individual need not be alone or without support whilst at work, and that a union could do so much for a worker or a group of workers if the need arose
.

Initially it was my shop steward, Dick Van Hagan, who invited me to a meeting of the Junior Workers Committee (JWC), a branch of the union. The committee met each month in the Blenheim Rooms, which was almost above the Blenheim Bar at the top of London Road. The JWC was a committee made up of apprentices from the various factories within the Edinburgh area which discussed issues affecting apprentices.

I found the meeting to be of real interest and I became very active; over the period of the next two years, I became minute secretary, secretary and eventually chairman of the JWC. It was at these meetings I learnt about meeting procedures and how to formulate resolutions and the beginnings of how to debate. I also got to know the difference between right and left wing in the political and union terms, and encountered apprentices who were communists and international socialists. As I was to the right wing in union terms, I soon locked horns with the communists and international socialists within the JWC. We had some great debates and arguments and I used to joke with them that, apart from their political beliefs, they were decent fellows. I could never understand their logic that to progress, the workers had to strike, upset the status quo and view the employers as a group to be overthrown and ruled by the workers. My view at that time was that workers, and the public in general, preferred stability and gradual change.

It was at a JWC dinner that I made my first speech and in some respects it was a disaster. I had decided to write my speech and basically just read it out to the audience. But on the night of the dinner, I was quite nervous and as I began to deliver my speech I noticed that, to my horror, the pages were out of order and I had to abruptly stop until I corrected the page sequence. The seconds that took seemed like hours to me and I never ever worked off written speeches again. Instead I preferred to memorise my speeches and back them up with headers.

I attended the National Conference of the JWC at Brighton in England to move a resolution opposing any return to conscription or national service in the United Kingdom and the next day I got a great kick from reading a very small note in the local press about the resolution being passed. It was at the JWC that I first met Pat Conner who was the AEU regional organiser; he was responsible for promoting and supporting Junior Workers' Committees throughout Scotland. Pat, who was from the west of Scotland, was a great support to me and the rest of the committee, and his love of his job and the union certainly rubbed of on me. I always thought that Pat would have made a good priest as he was a good listener and he always seemed to me to have a smile on his face.

During this period, I was also active in my local union branch which was the Edinburgh South Branch, No. 2. I also became friendly with Jack Keddie, the full-time Edinburgh district secretary of our union and another great source of help and encouragement to me during my time with the JWC. Due to the resignation of the Leith No.2 branch secretary, Jack Keddie asked me if I would be prepared to take over as part-time secretary of that branch. It was during the later stages of my father's illness, but I decided to give it a try. My father was pleased that I had taken on this part-time job.

By accepting this position, I became one of the youngest branch secretaries in the union at that time; I was only 22 years of age and had only just completed my apprenticeship. It was a position that I held for almost two years; I held it up until the Leith branches were amalgamated and I was able to resign. I was greatly helped and trained by the branch secretary of my previous branch, Jock McKinnon. He was a gruff no-nonsense sort of person, hard on the outside but tender on the inside and someone who I admired a lot. I used to visit his house every Wednesday for some training and his wife always provided a home-baked supper of cakes and scones and we used to have a great blether. They did not have a family and I am sure they both looked forward to Wednesday evenings, as I did.

One night, Jock was relating a story of how he had been travelling on an Edinburgh tram on Princes Street when a little girl ran in front of the tram and became trapped. The passengers and police all tried to get her out but she died before being freed. As Jock related the story he broke down and cried. His wife said that even though it had happened when Jock was a young man, he'd never been able to overcome this experience and always broke down when he recalled it.

It was around this time that I attended a union summer school for one week. This took place at Ruskin College, which was part of Oxford University and situated in Oxford, England. It was a wonderful week with glorious weather, great company and a bit of punting up the river during our free time. I met other young trade unionists from other parts of the United Kingdom and we spent our nights drinking beer and trying to solve all the political problems of the world. It was a great experience for me, meeting people from different walks of life and from different trade unions, and by being lectured in trade union topics and the past and future of trade unions by very experienced tutors. Forty plus years later, I sometimes reflect on that week in my life as today trade union membership has dropped dramatically and unions struggle to adapt to changing circumstances both politically and in the work place.

Chapter 19

On the 3rd of September 1965, having completed my apprenticeship, I left James H Lamont and started work at Ferranti as a turner in their Electronic Systems Machine Shop. My weekly wage was 14 Pounds, 6 shillings and 8 pence plus piecework. Piecework payments were a bonus. This simply meant that if you could produce more components than a set average, then you would be paid more and this could dramatically increase your wages.

At this time there was an exodus of young tradesmen from Lamont's to other companies as there were a number of jobs available elsewhere; the American company, Hewlett-Packard, had opened at Glenrothes in Fife, Cameron Iron Works had a large factory in Livingston and the BMC Motor Company operated a large plant at Broxburn. Ferranti Ltd. was also employing people and was desperate to entice tradesmen to their factory at Crewe Toll in Edinburgh. I was reluctant to apply for a job there as I was not sure that the work we did at Lamont's was as skilled as would be required at Ferranti; Ferranti manufactured navigation systems for planes such as the Harrier, Nimrod and F111 which were used by various countries as part of their defence capabilities.

But I decided to take the plunge on the basis that I would learn more and hopefully become more skilled. I also felt that by working at Ferranti, it could help my union prospects in the long term as Ferranti employed over 3,000 people in their various factories around Edinburgh. There was the main factory at Crewe Toll, one at Silverknowes and another at Granton, as well as a factory at Dalkeith. The company ran a shuttle service between the factories; this was for moving staff and mail deliveries. Later, during my time at Ferranti, they opened another factory at Robertson Avenue.

Ferranti was initially based in Manchester, England but it built the Crewe Toll factory during World War Two to manufacture Gyro Gun Sights for the R A F. The Crewe Toll factory was opened in 1943, and its wartime output was mainly used to equip the guns of Lancaster, Spitfire and Hurricane aircrafts. In a secret memo issued after the war, the Gyro Gun Sights was described as, "The single most important equipment introduced during the war". The factory was considered important enough to merit its own air defences, and an anti-aircraft rocket battery was sited next to it on Ferry Road.

My first day at Ferranti was an eye-opener. The buildings covered such a large area and the canteen catered for hundreds of people a day and had a menu which would have put some of Edinburgh's better restaurants to shame. Everything in the various departments and walkways was so clean and tidy, and the first aid room was really a surgery which was efficiently run by an experienced nursing sister called Sister Muir.

I was surprised to meet so many people who knew me from my work with the union and who came up to speak to me to make me feel welcome. One of those people was Arthur Hunter whom I had known when I was much younger, when he was an officer in the 35th Boys' Brigade. Arthur, who had strong Christian beliefs, was also chairman of the Ferranti Shop Stewards' Committee as well as being an ardent Hearts supporter. It was Arthur who later helped me get a season ticket for the centre stand at the Hearts Stadium at Tynecastle as, when the person who sat next to him in the centre stand died, Arthur let me know and I wrote asking to be considered to purchase the seat when it became available. A season ticket was almost impossible to purchase and I was very lucky to eventually get the seat. As a result, Arthur and I enjoyed our Saturday afternoons having a blether and watching 'the Jam Tarts'.

My first few days at Ferranti were spent being inducted into the system. Then I was taken to the electronic systems department machine shop where I was to work. There I was introduced to the manager of the department, Archie Nottman. I was then allocated to a machine, which was a Herbert No.7 Turret Lathe; it was one the likes of which I had never seen before.

I have to say that up to this stage I felt very comfortable about being at Ferranti as it seemed to be a good place to work and everyone was very friendly and helpful. My big concern was whether I would be able to do the work and, in that regard, I was fortunate over the next few weeks to make friends with Ruby Dickson, the female inspector who checked my work, and Ron Birch who was the machine setter who helped people out if there were problems during the manufacture of their components. And there was also Arthur Rowley, the leading hand who was an Englishman and crazy Hearts supporter; he knew my capabilities and used to give me the easier jobs. Without these people, I doubt if I would have survived in the early stages of my time there.

Fortunately fate was also to lend a hand and, within two months, the direction of my working life at Ferranti was to take a different turn. In November each year, shop stewards were elected from the various departments and after the election would join the Ferranti Shop Stewards' Committee which was a confederation of six different trade unions represented at Ferranti. There were over sixty shop stewards within Ferranti, and from this group a Works Council of seven Shop Stewards would be elected to form a negotiation team which would meet with management to discuss matters affecting the union membership. I was approached by a number of my workmates and asked to stand for the position of shop steward as the current shop steward had decided to resign. Whilst I did feel a little bit embarrassed about standing for the position, having only worked at Ferranti for just over two months, I decided to do so and at a lunchtime meeting in the department with everyone standing around the machinery, I was elected unopposed for the position of shop steward. I was 23 years of age.

The Monday following my election I attended my first Shop Stewards' Committee meeting. It was held during company time at four pm and lasted until five pm. At this meeting, the convener and vice-convener were elected, as was the Works Council and also the chairman of the Shop Stewards' Committee and the minute secretary. The structure of the shop stewards meeting was that they were held the first Monday of each month, and the minute secretary would provide an agenda. The chairman of the Shop Stewards' Committee would then run the meeting and the convener would be called to report on his workload from the previous month. There would then be questions and comments from those at the meeting, then the decisions and votes taken were recorded. All was done in a very professional and organised manner. The minutes were then typed up by the Ferranti typing pool and distributed around the factory ensuring that everyone was aware of the discussions at the meeting. It should be recognised that Ferranti, at this time, was way ahead of other employers in the district regarding their approach to industrial relations and to trade unions. There certainly was no other employer, to my knowledge, which allowed their employees to attend shop steward meetings during company time and then type out the minutes for distribution. Although trade union membership was approximately 95% of the workforce, it was not compulsory, and management would always support an employee who did not want to join the union even if that person was enjoying the benefits of the conditions negotiated between the union and the company.

Chapter 20

Three months after starting work at Ferranti, my father died. It took me a good six months to get my life back to normal after living with and looking after my father for so long. I was fortunate to be working at Ferranti during this part of my life as there were always things happening outside of work. There was an active social club which held regular dances and there was also a soccer team which I used to watch on a Saturday afternoon. Our department also had a ten-pin bowling team which I used to play for on a weekly basis.

Ron Birch was also a great help at this time and I became very friendly with him and his wife Phyllis. Ron had previously worked on the railways and was sure he had met my father during his short time there. Ron lived just up the road from me: above the fish and chip shop on Montrose Terrace.

Over the next two years, I gradually moved into other positions within the union and became a member of the District Committee which basically handled the running of the union for the Edinburgh district. It also communicated the national policy of the union to the local membership. The committee was made up of delegates from the local branches and meetings were held fortnightly, on a Wednesday, at the union office in the Blenheim Rooms situated at the top of London Road.

During this time I was moving up into key positions within the Ferranti Shop Stewards' Committee. I had served as minute secretary, and by the time I had reached 25 years of age, I was vice-convener and a member of the Works Council. At this stage, I would spend half of the week being booked onto union business, and the rest of the week I would be working on my machine. It was during this period that I got to know the various managers at Ferranti; I was able to watch their negotiating skills and get to know their good and bad points as negotiators. At the same time, I was also able to learn negotiating techniques from the convener of shop stewards as I was with him at most of the important meetings held with management.

I became convener of shop stewards in an unexpected manner. The current convener, Bill Sword, had been off work sick for at least three months. In his absence, as vice-convenor, I took over as acting convener. Bill was a semi-skilled process worker who had worked himself up through the Shop Stewards' Committee to become shop steward convener. He was very well liked by the membership and especially by most of the shop stewards. He was a fiery public speaker who gave the impression of being very militant and anti-management. But during our day-to-day meetings with management, I knew this not to be the case because as in most disputes solutions need to be found, and whilst fiery speeches may formulate the perception of a person, they mean nothing in the decision-making process of a dispute.

A day or so before Bill was due back to work, I was approached by a close friend of his who told me that he was going to report Bill to management and to our union District Committee. He alleged that Bill had gambling and alcohol problems and that he had taken money collected for an ex-Ferranti employee who had fallen on hard times in Australia, and had not sent any money on to that person. On Bill's return to work, he was approached by this friend and told that if he did not resign his position as convener, and concentrate on his health and family, then his friend would report these allegations to management and the union. I was not privy to the discussions between the two, but Bill gave his notice of resignation and left Ferranti that morning. And by this act he left a vacancy for the position of convener of shop stewards.

As acting convener I then had the difficult job of convening a meeting of the Works Council to explain that Bill had resigned. I also had to explain the alleged accusations. Most of the members were dumbstruck and did not believe the accusations, and I am sure that they felt that it was some grab for power by me. I was asked why I did not stop Bill from leaving until he had a chance to talk to the Works Council members. By this stage other shop stewards and union members throughout Ferranti were hearing a rumour that Bill had left, and shop stewards were demanding a meeting to discuss the matter. I knew that as a Works Council we had to resolve our own internal differences before we met the shop stewards and to this end, I asked the person accusing Bill to speak to the Works Council members and to be open and honest about his accusations. He agreed and it was a difficult and emotional meeting, but after his explanation, the members of the Works Council accepted that as Bill had left, they would let the matter rest. As a result, I arranged a meeting of the Shop Stewards' Committee for later that day and, after another difficult meeting, I was elected convener of shop stewards. This was to be a very difficult job, especially as I was so young, but I felt that I was ready for the job having served an apprenticeship within the union and having held most of the part-time positions. On top of that, I was well known, and I believe respected, for my union work both in the Edinburgh District and in Ferranti. From the beginning I made up my mind that I would lead rather than be lead, and as chief representative and spokesman for over 3,000 workers, I had to learn to exercise this considerable power in a responsible manner.

One of the first disputes I had as a shop steward before I became convener was over excessive heat in our machine shop. A number of the younger members wanted to walk out on strike because it was too hot. However, management were unable to control the heat, as there were heat wave conditions outside, but they were happy for people to leave their machines if need be and to drink as much water as possible. They also placed large fans around the workplace but this did not satisfy everyone. I was asked to call a meeting and the upshot was that the department did go out on strike because the management could not keep the machine shop cool.

I learnt a lesson that day which was that if you do not speak up against those pushing a different position, you will invariably find that the more level-headed people tend not to speak up. The result being that the wrong outcome is achieved. As the shop steward on that occasion, I allowed the membership to make the running as they were entitled to do, but did not offer alternative solutions which basically allowed the hotheads - excuse the pun - to dominate the meeting. However, another concern was that management may perceive the shop steward to be weak and one who raises frivolous complaints; the result of which could be that they may not take genuine complaints seriously. Anyway, the strike only lasted that day as the next day was cold with back-to-normal weather conditions and the grievances were forgotten. But from that day onward I changed my approach, and at meetings where there were differences of opinions, I always debated the issues and gave my point of view as well as that of the union's position, even if it made me unpopular amongst certain union members. All of this was good training for my future years as convener.

As the convener, shop stewards and Works Council were elected annually each November, I realised that I needed to consolidate my position during the coming year and so I began to work very hard to ensure that people got to know me. I had a number of early successes which helped me gain the support of those shops stewards who were concerned about my ability and the fact that I was very young to be a convener of shop stewards. I also felt that management were beginning to realise that, whilst I was firm in my negotiations with them, I was also prepared to compromise if it was in the best interest of both parties. I was on the right wing politically within the trade union movement and therefore did not believe that strike action was necessarily the best outcome in pursuit of an objective or improved working conditions. It should only be used as a last resort. As such, during my years as convener, we did not participate in any factory-wide strike action and it was generally accepted, apart from a difficult period in April 1972, that industrial relations between the Shop Stewards' Committee and

Ferranti management was a model for other engineering companies in the district.

The AEU had also changed during this period. In 1967, the National Union of Foundry Workers joined the AEU and became the Amalgamated Engineering and Foundry Workers Union (AEF) and, in 1970, the union merged with the Construction Workers and Draftsmen Unions to become the Amalgamated Union of Engineering Workers Union (AUEW) which would have taken the membership of the amalgamated union to around 1.3 million members.

When I joined the union, the president was Sir William Carron who was to the right politically. He was replaced in 1967 by the former communist, Hugh Scanlon. Hugh Scanlon was born in Melbourne, Australia but had moved to Manchester with his mother at the age of two after the death of his father. He started work as an apprentice instrument maker, and as an adult worked at Metro Vickers where he was shop steward before being elected as works convener of the plant. He won the presidency of the AEU from the Labour stalwart and AEU Scottish Executive full-time official, John Boyd, and was elevated to the House of Lords in 1979. And whilst I was a supporter of John Boyd, I found Hugh Scanlon to bring an exciting edge to union life at that time as he was so much more charismatic and challenging than his predecessor Sir William Carron.

John Boyd was the son of a miner who had spent most of his union life fighting left wing unionists from gaining control of the union. He commenced his career as an engineering worker and became an AEU union organiser in 1946. He was a very able speaker who, if I recall correctly, had a lilting Aryshire accent which made you want to listen. He was also a member of the Salvation Army and spent a lot of his time helping those in need. I remember on one occasion hearing him speak at a Burns Supper in Edinburgh to celebrate the anniversary and life and times of the great Scottish poet, Robert Burns. His understanding of Burns was profound and, apart from being very entertaining, his speech was very educational for those who did not know the history of Robert Burns. John Boyd was knighted in 1979.

The AEU was in many ways a very democratic union as the policy of the union was decided by the National Committee. Policy was decided by 52 rank and file delegates chosen by the various district committees throughout the country. These delegates would be from the left or right wing, and were generally closely matched in voting patterns. During my time, the right wing just had the edge in numbers. The outcome of this was that irrespective of the political leanings of the president of the union, the president had to vigorously support and, where possible, enact the policy of the National Committee.

When I attended National Committee in Eastbourne in 1971, I was only 29 years of age and a boy amongst men. Although I had a lot of experience and had held most part-time union positions since I was 17 years of age, I was silently in awe of the other members of the committee who were mostly middle-aged conveners, district presidents or branch secretaries with vast trade union experience. It was at National Committee that I was asked by John Boyd to be part of a small union delegation to visit Brussels to meet with European Common Market officials in order to discuss aspects of the common market which would affect trade unionists in the United Kingdom. At that time there was much talk about the UK joining the common market, and there was a lot of lobbying going on between those in favour and those against joining. I always remember that the flight from London to Brussels, gave me a life-long dislike of flying as we flew on a Trident aircraft the windows of which seemed to drop down to waist height and, whilst for some the view would have been exhilarating to me, it just made my feet tingle and my heart pound.

Chapter 21

Ferranti was built beside the suburb of Pilton, a working-class housing estate. Pilton had many social problems ranging from alcohol and some drug abuse, to poverty and unemployment. There were also other serious problems concerning young people which were caused by disadvantage and a lack of facilities. I felt that as a union, we had a responsibility to the local community where many of our members lived. And after being approached by a local councillor, I suggested to the Shop Stewards' Committee that we should broaden our activities from the workplace to the local community. It was agreed that we would organise a fund-raising project to purchase a mini-bus for the Ratho Youth Retreat in support of Pilton's youth. So we held a meeting with the shop stewards at the factory, and it was agreed to organise a fund-raising program and the Ferranti Employees Pilton Retreat Fund was set up with me as chairman. With tremendous support from the shop stewards and the workers at Ferranti, we organised a factory collection, a dance, a folk concert, a raffle and an Easter fair at the Old Kirk's Hall in Pennywell Road, Pilton. The proceeds from all of the functions were 400 Pounds, and we were very pleased with the result which went a long way to ensuring that the bus could be bought. To this day, the retreat is still in existence, and it is good to think that the efforts of the workers at Ferranti played some part in this great concept in support of Pilton's youth.

The minister of the Old Kirk of Edinburgh, West Pilton was the Reverend Colin Anderson who lived with his wife and children in the manse which was a part of the Old Kirk. The Old Kirk was totally white and was a landmark for the people of Pilton, but I always thought of it as a beacon for all those in need of help and there were many that were to benefit from the help and compassion shown by Colin Anderson. Colin was also the Industrial Chaplain for Ferranti and I got to know him very well during my years as convener. Even today we maintain contact.

Colin was very supportive during our fundraising efforts and also during the difficult periods when there was tension between management and unions. I can still remember seeing Colin's white collar and grey shirt standing out in the crowd when I was addressing a very large meeting held outside the grounds of Ferranti. It was gratifying, and in some ways humbling, that he would decide to show his support for the workers by attending the meeting. I should not have been surprised as Colin is a man of integrity and courage who always stands up for what he believes, even if it makes his life more difficult.

I remember seeing his photo on the front page of a local newspaper. He was playing football on a Pilton oval on a Sunday afternoon with a bunch of disadvantaged teenagers. In the 1960s the Church of Scotland was still a bit puritanical, and I am sure Colin would have been criticised by some quarters for his actions. I remember seeing him nursing a black eye on one occasion. It may have been as a result of an altercation with a wife-beating husband or a person high on alcohol, or even perhaps an injury obtained playing football. In any event, I did not ask and was not told, such was the stature of the man.

Colin also encouraged me to give talks on industrial topics at his men and youth's group meetings, on some occasions I was joined by the Ferranti Personnel Manager, Jim Wright who was a very able and sincere man. On one occasion, at Colin's request, I pre-recorded a talk for radio on the relevance of Trade Unionism and Religion in working life, which was part of a church broadcast on BBC Scotland. Colin also helped me in my efforts to improve my education. I had recently passed the 'O' level English exam, but needed help if I was to pass Higher English. When Colin heard of this, he spoke to one of his parishioners who was a teacher and this lady worked with me during a year of night classes. I was very pleased indeed to pass Higher English with an above average pass. This pleasure was intensified given the difficulty I had had at primary and secondary school in passing exams.

During this period, my next-door neighbour Mr Elder became very ill and I would take Mrs Elder up to the hospital by car and on some occasions, if Mrs Elder was tired, I would visit on my own. I remember on one evening climbing up the stairs of the hospital with Mrs Elder when I began feeling out of breath and out of condition. The next day I went to the first aid room at work and Sister Muir weighed me. I was just under seventeen stone and realised that since my father's death, because of my increased union work, I had been eating on the run and thus had been having too much fried food and alcohol. I immediately went on a diet and, over a period, I eventually got back to my more normal weight of around thirteen and a half stone.

Mr Elder died after a short time in hospital and as Mrs Elder did not have any other living relatives other than Mr Elder's relatives, she asked me to help her arrange the funeral. After the funeral, which was held in the morning, I suggested that I take her out for lunch. We went to a local Chinese restaurant, which was on our way home, which she enjoyed immensely as she had never been to one before. During the meal she said that as Mr Elder was now dead and there was no one left in her family, she wanted to leave me her house when she eventually died. I was a bit embarrassed about it and did not know what to say, but she said that she would contact her solicitor in the morning to organise it. This she did as I was summonsed by her Solicitor a few weeks later to meet with him and sign some papers.

Chapter 22

In my second year as convener, I had to lead the negotiations for a new three-year agreement. One of the issues I raised with the Works Council members was the need for us to go on the offensive and challenge management to look at their wage structure in order to reduce the number of wage rates, as well as how they evaluated job rates for the actual work. We were keen to have higher set rates plus bonuses for those workers who worked on piecework. A number of the Works Council members were against the idea of a job evaluation as they felt it would be difficult to sell to the membership. They thought that the different trades would believe that they should be on the top of the evaluation with the best rates of pay. I argued that if the rates of pay set against the new grades were realistic, then people would vote to accept them. The end result was that the Works Council agreed to the job evaluation proposal although we all agreed that we would need to work hard to get any offer accepted and that it would not be easy.

The negotiations were made more difficult when management, whilst prepared to consider a form of job evaluation, wanted the employees to therefore increase productivity and to give up their morning and afternoon ten-minute breaks as part of the increase in wages offered. They proposed that the trolley service would be replaced by food and beverage vending machines which could be used by workers on an 'as required basis'. This on the whole meant that if the proposal was accepted, we would no longer be able to queue up at break time to be served by the canteen trolley ladies and their trolleys of freshly-made tea and coffee, bacon, black pudding rolls and cakes.

After weeks of negotiations I met with our members at the canteen in the Crewe Toll factory. The canteen was overflowing and the other Works Council members and I were squashed into one corner of the room with a table and microphone. There would have been over 1,000 people in attendance, such was the interest. I advised the meeting that we had finalised an agreement, which we felt was worth supporting and I then spent the next hour explaining the concept of the agreement and the monetary payments offered. The members were then told that the shop stewards would meet with their members in their own departments to discuss how it would affect each individual department and trade. A healthy majority eventually carried the proposed contract and I was very pleased with the outcome.

Chapter 23

Perhaps the most difficult period during my time as convener was the dispute and strike involving the machine tool maintenance department. The dispute had its origins in the previous works agreement, which did not evaluate the Machine Tool Fitters (MTF) within the top classification as they were classified as Class 2. For a number of months we had been in discussion with management about changing the MTF from Class 2 to Class 1, but were unable to convince them that they deserved to be upgraded. We persuaded the MTF to go through the normal dispute procedures as we pursued their claim with management.

At this stage a minority Socialist group were very vocal in their newsletters about the way the shop stewards conducted union business at Ferranti. Their newsletter, which was handed out at the various Ferranti sites around Edinburgh, subjected me in particular to some personal abuse. My view was that as a union we should consider ways to stop them making incorrect statements and trying to interfere in the decision-making process of our members. The tough and skilful divisional organiser of the AUEW, Ernie Leslie, who was very much from the right of the union movement was sympathetic and we met with our union solicitors in Falkirk. Unfortunately, whilst the solicitor agreed that we had a case, he felt that it would cost time and money to pursue and that it would only give them more front-page exposure. I was disappointed with the outcome and continued to rebuff their comments wherever possible. In hindsight our solicitors were correct. By taking them head on we would have only played into their hands by giving them the publicity they craved.

After many months, the MTF got frustrated with the dispute procedures and went out on strike. By this stage I had persuaded the Shop Stewards' Committee that we should organise a weekly collection from other union members, rather than try to get other departments to strike in support of the MTF. My reason for this approach was that I did not believe other departments would agree to strike as they would not gain personally by their actions, and by this method, we would contain the dispute within the MTF department. I never felt that the MTF had the total support of other union members and was determined that the strike would not spread to other departments and fall apart because of a lack of unified support. With this method, we had some control over the dispute and at least knew that it would not spread. It was a good negotiating technique as we were seen to be trying to contain the dispute. During this period the support of the shop stewards was impressive as money had to be collected, counted, processed and given to the MTF each week. We also received money from other union members including the shipbuilding workers on the Clydeside in Glasgow who had heard of the dispute and wanted to help.

Eric Mason, who was vice-convener, was immensely helpful during this period and set up a system to streamline the payments to the MTF. I can still see him in my mind's eye, sitting and counting the collection for distribution. Eric was also the branch secretary of the Tollcross Branch of the Amalgamated Engineering Union, and was later to become one of the longest serving part-time branch secretaries in the union, as well as a Justice of the Peace.

The dispute which took a turn for the worse after I informed management that I intended to address a meeting of our members at the Robertson Avenue factory car park, to discuss the progress of the dispute in the afternoon of the next day, April 15th, 1972.

Just before getting ready to leave for the meeting, I was approached by a legal clerk. He handed me an interim interdict: a legal document which basically meant that if I, or other shop stewards, attended or addressed the meeting we would be in contempt of court and could be jailed or fined. One of the reasons for this put forward by management, was that if the meeting had gone ahead, employees' cars could have been damaged because of the numbers attending the meeting. At that time there was a view that Ferranti management were encouraged by the policies of the Heath Government who favoured a Prices and Incomes Policy which was opposed by the Trade Union Movement. Later, in 1973, a coalminer's work-to-rule led to power cuts and a three-day working week. Whilst there may have been national industrial unrest and concern within the trade union movement during this time, I believe the decision taken by management was purely site-based and not because of external influences or government policy pressures. Management, I felt, was frustrated and hamstrung because of the success of our actions up to that point and was desperate to be seen to take a stand against our claim.

By recourse to law, their actions were very radical at the time and could have had far reaching consequences throughout industry nationally if I, or one of our shop stewards, had been jailed. My first reaction was of disbelief that the management would take this form of action. Over the past few years the industrial relations within the factory had gone from good to very good, and there had always been a feeling of mutual trust between the current Shop Stewards' Committee and the management team. By their action, management was in danger of undoing all the good work that had been achieved during the life of the factory.

I decided that I would cancel the meeting at Robertson Avenue as I felt to go ahead with it would not be in our interest as we would be breaking the law. Our dispute was not with the Court but with Ferranti management who had in our opinion overreacted.

When it became known around the various Ferranti factories, there was uproar and shop stewards were being urged to organise mass walkouts in protest. At the same time that this was occurring, local and national newspaper reporters who sensed a big story in the making were pursuing me. By three o'clock, I had organised a meeting of the Works Council to decide on a recommendation to put forward to a meeting of the Shop Stewards' Committee at four o'clock. The meeting with the shop stewards was emotional, and at times fiery, with calls for all sorts of boycotts and strike action, but we eventually managed to get everyone to agree that we first organise a meeting with the top managers from Ferranti. It was also agreed that the full-time organisers of the various unions would contact management to complain about their tactics. I also used the media, both locally and nationally, to criticise the decision to serve interdicts on myself and the other shop stewards.

Eric Mason and I eventually met with Donald MacCallum who was the Group General Manager for Ferranti, Scotland. We had afternoon tea with chocolate cake in a very relaxed setting in his large office. Given what had happened over the past two days, tea and sympathy would have been more appropriate. Donald MacCallum was a very pleasant and reasonable person who seemed keen to resolve the problem and move on. Eric and I put forward our views quite strongly, but we both knew that we needed to move on and continue to concentrate on the dispute that caused the serving of the interim interdicts. Nevertheless, Eric made a good point during our meeting when he said in an indignant manner, "You even sent the interdict to me when I was away for the week at a union course in England and not even in the country".

The MTF strike eventually ended when management agreed to our claim to make their job Class 1. The dispute did not ultimately damage relations between union and management; cool heads on both sides ensured that good industrial relations would continue well into the future.

Chapter 24

It was around this time that I became involved with the Ferranti Thistle Soccer Team.

Alan Hartman and John Miekle who had both helped run the team had decided to retire and they asked me if I would be interested in taking over from them. The team played in the Under 21 Juvenile League and whilst they were not a bad side, they had never won a trophy. I agreed to become manager of the team and began looking for a coach. Ian Brown who used to work at Lamont's and who had had some trial games with the Hearts had joined Ferranti as an Inspector and agreed to come on board to coach the team. He was a great asset as he was a very good coach. We then persuaded another Ferranti employee, George Shaw, to train the team. George had been part of the training team of the great Scottish boxing champion Kenny Buchanan.

Also on our committee were Jimmy Miller, who worked for Ferranti at the Silverknowes factory. The last member of our committee was old Willie Batten who was our masseur. Willie would have been over 75 years old. He was a real character that never missed a game even though he did have problems running onto the field when the players got injured; he always got a great cheer from the sideline when he got back from tending to the player. Willie was a tough nut. I remember as we were getting out of my car at Silverknowes prior to a game, the car door got caught in a blast of wind and slammed shut on Willie's thumb leaving it partially severed.

His reaction was to wrap it up in a handkerchief and ask me to drive him to hospital. Apparently Willie worked with the ambulance corp during World War One and had to hold soldier's heads together during operations so was used to the sight of blood.

Some of my jobs at the club were to sign up new players and look after the current ones, as well as ensuring that the team was financially viable and that a training ground and equipment were made available. Our plan was to try to break the bogey of not winning a trophy in the league and I spent a lot of time trying to persuade some of the better juvenile players in Edinburgh to join our team. Our facilities were very good which helped persuade a few key players to join our team.

It was a very happy period in my life as both the players and the committee shared a great amount of team spirit and we used to all have a great time after the game on Saturday afternoons. We had a great blend of players; a few of them worked for Ferranti and the rest came from various backgrounds and they all got on well with each other.

Some of the players I remember were Geoff Skeldon who was our goalkeeper; he worked for Ferranti and lived in Pilton. And apart from being a good goalie, he had a tremendous affinity with the team possibly because of his connections to Ferranti and Pilton. In the team we also had two civil servants, Graeme McArthur and David Atkinson, who joined us after playing with the Salveson Boys' Club U17 side. Other players I recall were Alex Carse, a student, and Tommy McKenzie, named after his father the great Heart of Midlothian full-back. I remember taking Tommy up to Perth one evening to play a trial game for St Johnstone who played in the then first division of the Scottish Football League.

Chapter 25

It was also at this time that I met my future wife, Roslyn Savage. She was on a working holiday from her home in Brisbane, Australia. She worked in the Personnel Department of Ferranti and I used to see her when I would visit the Female Personnel Manager on union business. She was a very attractive woman with a happy outgoing personality; I still remember her wearing a long brown skirt and a flowing yellow blouse and long leather boots. She also looked extremely healthy sporting what remained of her Australian tan.

One Friday evening, I attended a dance at the Ferranti Social Club mainly because there would be a late night alcohol license which allowed for drinks after ten pm. Roslyn and her friend Myra, who was eventually Roslyn's best maid at our wedding, was there and I struck up a conversation with them. On the Wednesday after the dance, I was waiting for the bus at Crewe Toll after work when I noticed Roslyn walk by. She had walked a good bit further up the road when I decided to run after her and ask her out. When I caught up with her we walked and talked together until we reached her lodgings at Stockbridge. There I asked her if she would like to go to the Prudential Insurance dance with me. Roslyn accepted and that was the beginning of a whirlwind romance which was to result in our marriage seven months later. We had a great night at the dance and after that spent most of our time together.

We always joke about our first meals together. I remember inviting Roslyn to my place and making her sliced sausages, fried in a pan with tomatoes, which were cooking in the sausage grease; hardly a good setting for romance. Roslyn, on our first dinner at her flat at Warrender Park Crescent, was more health conscious. I had arrived early and was knocking at her door when she came running up the stairs with an enormous cabbage and a tin of Fray Bentos corned beef. She shared the flat with three or four other girls and as a result it was an obstacle course to walk around as there were clothes hanging up to dry everywhere from the kitchen to the lounge room. It was then that I ceased to believe that all girls were tidy.

Roslyn loved coming to the Ferranti Thistle soccer games and she quickly got to know all of the players. She learned the rules of soccer and developed a lifetime interest in the game.

When Roslyn and I had met in March, she had told me then that she had a ticket to go home to Australia in September. In May, she left for a two-week holiday to Italy and while she was away, I took some time to consider our relationship. Whilst I did not want our friendship to end in September, I did not know how our relationship could continue as I did not want to leave Scotland.

I remember our first meeting after she came back from Italy. We had arranged to go to see the film, *Death in Venice* and met outside the Regal Cinema on Lothian Road. Roslyn turned up bearing gifts for me from Italy. One was a lovely red Italian shirt and the other was a porcelain drinking mug from a small Italian village. Unfortunately the shirt was just too small for me, but I still have the drinking mug to this day. I remember sitting in the cinema watching the film and listening to the beautiful and hauntingly sad Adagietto from Gustav Mahler's, *Symphony No. 5*, and wondering how I could persuade Roslyn to stay in Scotland. It was during this film that I began to think of marriage as the best option, if she would have me.

It was in July that year that I proposed to Roslyn, or should I say Roslyn proposed to me. We both had been reluctant to talk about Roslyn's impending departure back to Australia and the fact that she would be leaving soon. Roslyn said that she felt that I did not seem to care that she would be leaving. Given courage by the thought that Roslyn did not want to leave me, I told her that I did not want to lose her and asked if she would consider marrying me. I told Roslyn that I would never consider moving to Australia as I had no skills other than being a good trade union convener, something which I thought would be difficult to replicate in Australia. To my surprise Roslyn accepted my idea of marriage and this set off a very emotional few months as we both set about informing our families about our decision to get married.

The next morning I awoke with all sorts of trepidations. I wondered if Roslyn would phone to say the she had changed her mind. I also questioned how was I going to look after her as I did not have very much money. I took some consolation in knowing that we would be able to live in my house at Alva Place until we had saved enough money for a deposit on a house of our own. I was also concerned how Roslyn's parents would react to the fact that Roslyn had decided to make her home in Edinburgh with me and not return to Australia.

When we next met, Roslyn and I agreed that she would contact her parents to tell them of our plans to get married and that I would write them a letter telling them about myself. Roslyn later told me how difficult it was for her telling her parents of our plans during a phone call which in those days was made more difficult by the standard of telephone reception. A week or so after telephoning her parents, Roslyn received a letter from them saying that they had decided not to come over for the wedding, but that they would organise to come over a year later. We both appreciated that it was very hard for them to make the trip over at such short notice, but were buoyed by the fact that they would be coming over once we were settled. Roslyn was particularly happy about this. My family was very happy about our decision to get married as they all liked Roslyn. Our friends and workmates at Ferranti were all taken by surprise. It did indeed cause a minor sensation there at the time.

Now, as a parent myself, I can understand how Roslyn's parents must have felt when she told them that she was marrying a Scotsman whom they did not know, and was staying on to make her life in Edinburgh. They both must have been devastated;

more so as they had never met me and did not know my background or what type of person I was.

We agreed that we would have a church wedding and then hold a reception for forty people at the Minto Hotel in Newington. After paying for the wedding and reception, it would mean that we would start our life together with very little money in our little rented house in Abbeyhill.

One of the problems we had whilst arranging the wedding was who would take the place of Roslyn's father and escort her down the aisle. Roslyn was very happy when her bridesmaid, Myra Keller's father agreed to take her father's place. In normal circumstances my Uncle Frankie should have taken my father's place at the wedding, but instead I chose my Aunt Ada's husband, Uncle Alec. I had always been close to Uncle Alec, more so during the long period of my father's illness when he had been very supportive to me. He had also been my father's closest friend, and we all had some great times together over the years. As a youngster I used to admire the way he would become the life and soul of the party at our family gatherings. Sadly, he died a few months before we left for Australia. It was a short illness and I felt privileged to be one of those with him when he died.

Prior to the wedding, Uncle Frankie and Aunty Gracie came to visit and bring their wedding present and I was chastised by Aunty Gracie for not choosing Uncle Frankie to take the place of my father. This was the protocol as Uncle Frankie was my father's eldest brother. I could understand Aunty Gracie's feelings and explained my reasons for choosing Uncle Alec. I was glad that they accepted my explanation, especially as I did not want to upset Uncle Frankie.

A few weeks before the wedding, I told Mrs Elder that I was to be married and that I wanted her to come to the wedding. I explained that it would not change our friendship as Roslyn and I would always look after her. Unfortunately, almost from that day on, Mrs Elder took to her bed with illness, and a few days before the wedding she was taken to hospital. Whenever I went in to see her whilst she was in bed at home, she never spoke to me. She just lay there. Perhaps the news of my impending marriage hurt her and she lost her enthusiasm for living. And whilst she may have already been becoming ill, our news may have fast-tracked her illness. She died whilst Roslyn and I were on honeymoon at my mother's elderly Aunt Elizabeth's home in Findhorn. There we spent three lovely days after driving up from Edinburgh the morning after our wedding.

We were married on October 30th, 1971 at St Catherine's Argyle Parish Church. It was a cold day. Jack Johnston and David Reekie who were from the Personnel Department at Ferranti had offered to record the service on tape to send back to Roslyn's parents in Australia. Roslyn was thrilled about their offer and Jack and David hid in the church pulpit to record the service. We sent the tape to Australia but unfortunately her parents could not bear to listen to it as it upset them too much. At the reception, as my best man Willie Melrose read out the wedding telegrams, there wasn't one from Roslyn's parents, which really upset Roslyn. What had happened was that their telegram had been forwarded to the Glasgow telegram exchange by mistake and we received it with other mail when we returned from our honeymoon. Also on our return from our honeymoon, I received a letter from a firm of Edinburgh Solicitors advising me that Mrs Elder had left me her house. I was to attend their office to tidy up the paperwork which transferred the house to me. I also received a letter from the late Mr Elder's niece accusing me of stealing items from the house, and telling me that she would be claiming all the contents of the house and that I was not to enter the home until all the contents were removed. The letter was insulting and particularly upset Roslyn. Because of this, I took the letter with me to Mrs Elder's solicitor and asked him to write a reply telling Mr Elder's niece to refrain from writing to me in the future. I never heard anymore of the matter.

Chapter 26

During the first year of our marriage I decided that I would not stand as a delegate for the National Committee of the union as it meant being away from home for three weeks each year. I already spent two to three nights a week at meetings and felt that the time away from home was too much in the early stages of our marriage. My place on the National Committee was taken by a very good friend of mine, James McNicol, or 'Mac' as he was known. He was a widower and branch secretary of the Musselbourgh branch of the union. We were both members of the District Committee and the Divisional Committee of our union.

I recall, with fond memory, meeting Mac for lunch at the Café Royale restaurant just behind the Registry Office at the east end of Edinburgh before travelling to Divisional Committee meetings. Mac was liked by everyone and was famous for his sayings. When things were difficult at work, he used to say things like, "Don't worry – unduly". After closing time at the pub it was never, "Where is the nearest bus stop?" but "get me to the nearest shipping line". He was an accomplished featherweight boxer whilst he was in the Air Force, but used to jokingly tell everyone in the pub after a District Committee Meeting that if anyone gives you a problem, "Punch them and make sure that you run".

Mac died a few years after I left for Australia, but it is good to know that he is in a painting which hangs in the People's Story Museum in the Canongate Tollbooth on Edinburgh's Royal Mile. The painting was commissioned by the union to celebrate the move to new premises at Morrison Street, just up the road from Haymarket in Edinburgh. The painting depicts the then District Committee members walking in a union march under the union banner. I am also in the painting. I remember the artist Sandy Moffat meeting all of us to take our photograph which he then used to paint each member into the painting. Family members who have seen it say the likeness to me is very good. It is a very good painting and deserves to hang in the People's Story Museum as it portrays a proud part of Edinburgh's trade union history.

Chapter 27

About six months after our wedding, we received the keys and the deeds to Mrs Elder's house at 16 Alva Place. We then set about modernising it and were very lucky to get a grant from the Government which assisted with the updating of the house. It took over six months to complete, but this was made easier as we could walk away from the renovations to our home next door and did not have to live in a house where work was taking place.

Our first child, Graeme, was born whilst we were still in the old house and I still remember walking with Roslyn down to Elsie Ingles Maternity Hospital after she started to have contractions. The maternity hospital was only a ten-minute walk from home and it was a lovely warm summer evening in June. As we were walking down to the hospital, we met my Uncle Frankie who would have been nearing eighty years of age and very deaf. We tried to explain to him what was happening, but I was never really sure if Uncle Frankie understood. Still, it was good to see him nevertheless.

Uncle Frankie was very interested in the life of Sir Walter Scott and knew a great deal about this great Scottish writer. He was very good with words and at poetry. He had written poems about his brothers and sisters and his family life in general. Incidentally my father's youngest brother, Fred, who lived in South Africa was also a very good painter. I have a painting of an owl painted by Uncle Fred, which was given to me by my cousin Moira. It had been kept by Aunty Ada, Moira's mother, for many years before it came to me. It is good that the family trait from Uncle Fred has been passed down to our eldest son Graeme. Indeed he has also painted an owl, very similar to Uncle Fred's, that we have somehow misplaced.

Graeme was born on the 6th of June, 1972. I remember walking down to the hospital after work. I was so excited that I phoned the maternity hospital from just a block away and was told that Roslyn had given birth to a healthy baby boy. It must have been very difficult for Roslyn during the period before and after Graeme's birth as her family was so far away from her. Neither of us really knew a lot about babies and we still recall the nightmare of getting the right size of teat for the baby bottle; Graeme had a big problem with wind and we felt that we were the cause of the problem. We were lucky that Aunty Ada kept calling in as she would take Graeme out for long walks which allowed Roslyn to sleep and regain her strength. Aunty Ada was again a tower of strength, as she had been so much in the past, which helped Roslyn to recover after the birth.

When we moved into our newly renovated home, it was so much easier for us all. Although the house was small, it was very modern and had a beautiful bathroom and shower, something we had never experienced in our old house next door, which, incidentally, the owner could now take possession of after all these years.

Not long after moving into our own house, we received a letter from Roslyn's parents telling us that they would be coming over to Scotland to stay with us for a few weeks. This worried me because, although the house was very functional, it was still only a one bedroom home and there was no available room for Roslyn's parents to sleep. We agreed that we should move and I set about looking for a new and bigger house.

If I were to do now what I did then, buy a house which Roslyn had not seen, I would be shot at dawn. But that is basically what I did. I went out and found a house which I thought we would both like and bought it. The house was at Craiglea Crescent in Trinity, a well-regarded suburb that was a short walk from Trinity School and not far from my work at Ferranti. Trinity was also within walking distance from the old fishing port of Newhaven. As a young boy I well remember standing outside Middleton's pub watching the 'fisher wives' from Newhaven as they trudged up Easter Road to set up their mussel stalls. I was mesmerised watching the fisher wives; dressed almost totally in black, they carried their wares in a basket on their backs held by a strap across their forehead. Men would come out of the pub to have a saucer full of mussels and brine before going to the Saturday game to watch the Hibs. When they finished, the saucer was dipped into a pan of salt water ready to be used again. In winter when the air is clear and crisp the smell of mussels and salt water mixed with the smell of beer and fish and chips always reminds me of Saturdays and football and Easter Road.

Our new house was a large first-floor flat with two large bedrooms. The large front room looked out onto Edinburgh's Ruin, which was similar to the Parthenon in Greece, but it was often called 'Edinburgh's Disgrace' because at the time the Edinburgh Council ran out of money and was unable to finish the project. The ruin was floodlit on a number of occasions and, looking out from our window, was a spectacular site. The house was bought for 7,500 pounds and we were able to sell our home at Alva Place for a very good price of 5,000 pounds.

Whilst Roslyn quite liked the house, it quite possibly would not have been the house she would have chosen. However, it was really a *fait accompli* as I bought it on behalf of us both. After we moved in, the one thing that she did not appreciate was that she had to go downstairs to put the washing out in the back green and therefore had to take Graeme up and down with her each time. When our second son Stephen was born, she then had the added problem of looking after two boys whilst putting out the washing. Adding to this problem was the ritualistic system of taking the washing line down after the washing had dried and having to put it up again before putting more washing out. Woe betide anyone who had the temerity to buck the system and leave the washing line up as you would be invariably shouted at by the local 'witch' who would be leering from her window as some sort of self-appointed custodian of proper clothes hanging practices. Before Roslyn's parents arrived, we did some major renovations to our kitchen and soon we were all ship shape and ready for them.

We had a wonderful time with Roslyn's parents during their stay. I got on well with them and the weather was magnificent as it was dry and very warm. We drove up to the Black Isle for two weeks to let Roslyn's parents see a bit more of Scotland and they were intrigued to see a washing line hanging with clothes drying over the sea at full tide. This meant that the owners of the clothes would not get their clothes back until the tide went back out. It only emphasised the laid-back approach the locals had to life and made our holiday more memorable.

Just before Roslyn's parents left to go back to Australia, Roslyn's mother took her out to a shop opposite Kings Theatre to buy her a sewing machine. Roslyn's mother was determined that Roslyn should have one as she probably felt that she would never see her daughter again, and in a motherly way she was making sure that Roslyn had the tools she would need to help her clothe her family.

After a wonderfully happy six weeks, Roslyn's parents left by bus from St Andrews Square. They must have been emotional as they left us, but for Roslyn's sake they did not show it, Roslyn also did not show her emotions but I know that she was hurting at the time.

It was then that I started to think about my ultimatum to Roslyn when we decided to get married: that I would never go to live in Australia seemed unfair, arbitrary and unworkable.

Chapter 28

My last season with Ferranti Thistle was a very good one and we made the final of the Bob Tait Trophy and the East of Scotland Cup. We won the Bob Tait Trophy after drawing a game played at Tynecastle Park, and winning the replay at Saughton Enclosure. We decided to try to lift the players for the replay and organised lunch at the Hearts Supporters Club which was based at Tynecastle, and after lunch the players walked around to Saughton Enclosure to get ready for the game. This tactic seemed to have an effect on the players and they went on to win the first ever trophy for Ferranti Thistle. Jimmy Markie was the team captain that day. Our other final, which was The East of Scotland Cup, was also played at Saughton Enclosure on the following Saturday. It was a strange affair as we were winning 3-0 at half time but lost the game by losing six goals in the second half.

Our time with the soccer team was a great experience for both Roslyn and I and we made a lot of new friends amongst the players and the committee members. Apart from watching a few of the games, Roslyn also used to wash the football strips for the team. This was a terrible job, especially in the winter months when the strips would be covered in mud. We had a small washing machine which struggled to clean the thirteen strips, pants and socks, which most weeks had to be soaked first to get rid of the grass and dirt stains. She then worked most of the week trying to get them dry in time for the next game. We were fortunate that our strip was mainly dark in colour; the jersey had black and yellow stripes and the pants and socks were black.

Playing football in Edinburgh during the winter months was not for the faint-hearted as the weather could be dismal with rain, and sleet was a frequent companion. At half-time we would serve up hot tea and orange quarters, and on some occasions hot Bovril. After the game, the players would trudge back to the dressing room soaking wet and ready to fight for some space in the hot showers which were always crowded due to a number of other games being played at the same time. It was also a challenge for the committee members during the winter months as they stood on the touchline being battered by wind and rain with feet like blocks of ice.

On the Friday evening before a game it was normal to check the Edinburgh Evening News to find out if any of the corporation pitches were unplayable on the Saturday. This prevented teams from wasting time and money by going to the game. On the odd occasion, pitches were deemed unplayable an hour or so before the game. This would become a committee-person's nightmare because the players used to get really annoyed as their afternoon would be wasted and they would then have to make their way home without playing. But it would be wrong for me to imply that every Saturday was rainy or windswept. Some weekends were mild and sunny and I recall watching games at Inverleith Park or Leith Links on balmy spring evenings when the days were beginning to stretch out and it did not became dark until late in the evening.

Ferranti also had a senior team who played in the East of Scotland League. They were called Ferranti Thistle Football Club and were originally formed as a works team in 1943. Just before I left for Australia they gained selection into the Scottish Football League for the 1974-75 season and, if I recall correctly, they changed their name to Meadowbank Thistle Football Club and moved to Meadowbank Stadium which was situated not far from where my father finished his railway days as an engine driver at St Margaret's Shunting Yard.

Chapter 29

Late in 1973, Roslyn again fell pregnant. It was around this time that I was becoming a bit frustrated and unsettled. At a very young age I had done almost all of the part-time roles within the union and was always hoping that a full-time union position would become vacant. At this period there were no such positions on the horizon and I couldn't see any future opportunities for me.

In March 1974, on a cold Sunday morning, Roslyn and I were sitting in the front room of our house and I asked Roslyn if she would like to go back to Australia to live. By raising the subject the way I did, I knew that there would be no going back as it would have been cruel to raise Roslyn's hopes and then decide not to go. I knew that this was an offer Roslyn would embrace, albeit after she ensured that I was happy and felt comfortable about moving. I have to say that Roslyn had never, at any time up to that point in our marriage, shown any interest or spoken to me or anyone else about going back to live in Australia. Determined to set our decision in concrete, the next day I advised my shop stewards and Ferranti management that we would be moving to live in Australia later in the year.

My decision to leave Edinburgh to live in Brisbane had its origin in my initial decision to set the rules about our marriage by stating that I would never leave Edinburgh to live in Australia. I slowly came to the conclusion that, even if Roslyn was happy living in Edinburgh, it was unfair, unrealistic and wrong of me to expect Roslyn to accept it forever. The more I thought about it, the more unrealistic and unworkable it seemed and the guiltier I felt about it. I suppose it was then that I started to think about the more positive things about living in Australia. I felt that there would be better education and lifestyle opportunities for the boys in Brisbane. And also Roslyn would be nearer to her family which relieved the worry of what would happen if her parents took ill; how would she cope with not being able to help as distance between Scotland and Australia was a tremendous barrier?

Chapter 30

Whilst I have no regrets about moving to Australia, whether by fate or choice or chance, my spur-of-the-moment decision to move to Australia was one which I did not research enough. There were many aspects of this move which we never considered and which caught us both by surprise. I would certainly recommend that for one of the most important decisions in one's life, that people take time to consider all possible outcomes, the negatives as well as the positives, before making any decision. And whenever possible, it is always best to get used to the idea before making or announcing such a decision.

A few days after announcing that I would be leaving by the end of the year, the general secretary of the Amalgamated Union of Engineering Workers, Jim Conway, was killed in the Turkish Airlines DC10 which crashed near Paris on the 3rd of March, 1974 killing all 345 passengers. I had last seen Jim when he had visited Edinburgh to speak at a Work Study Conference arranged by Phil Swan who was the work study manager, and my opposite number at Ferranti. Phil Swan was a good man and a formidable opponent to me. After the conference, Roslyn and I were invited to dinner by Jim Conway. Ernie Leslie, the divisional organiser of the union, and his wife were also present.

Jim Conway was well respected, both in the United Kingdom and internationally, as a modern right-wing trade unionist. At the time that he died, he was in the process of computerising the union headquarters in London thus basically modernising the union. He had strong views and visions about things such as Trade Union Credit Unions and shops where members could buy cut-price goods and services etc. He also believed in having kindergartens in the workshops where women could leave their children whilst they were working. He was a great loss to the Trade Union Movement and particularly to the AUEW.

The following month, on April 26th, our second child, Stephen, was born at the Eastern General Hospital. Eric Mason and his wife had kindly offered to look after Graeme for us and I took Roslyn to the hospital late on the 25th and then waited by the telephone. Unfortunately, I fell asleep and when I phoned the hospital I was advised that Stephen had already been born. Stephen slept very well when he came home, but once he grew a little bit older we had to spend a lot of time taking him out for walks as he tended to cry a bit if he was not active.

One of my last jobs as convener was to be involved with the Duke of Edinburgh project. This brought young delegates from business and politics from around the world to discuss their activities from an international perspective. If I remember correctly, the delegates were housed in university lodgings and there were various visits and functions as well as speeches by well-known business people, politicians and trade unionists. I really enjoyed listening to the various speeches and meeting some of the delegates, one of whom was a young Australian Member of Parliament called Ian McPhee; he was later to become Ethnic Affairs Minister in the Fraser Government.

Ferranti was host to some of the delegates and I was asked to give a talk about our industrial relations and union structure at the factory as well as how we were able to manage more than six trade unions within the factory without any obvious breakdown in the decision-making process. I remember leaving the meeting very pleased with my presentation as it gave me a chance to talk about the things that the Shop Stewards' Committee had achieved during my six years as convener.

To celebrate my last job as convener of shop stewards - the election for the new convener was to take place the following Monday - I drove down to the Starbank Pub which was just down the road from our house in Trinity. As I looked out over the sea towards Fife, I raised my pint of beer and said to myself, "Well that's that then. It's over".

At the shop stewards meeting the following Monday, I officially resigned and thanked everyone for their help during my time as convener. Dougie Rooney who was vice-convener was elected convener and made a very gracious speech thanking me for the work I had put in over the years. Dougie was the first Ferranti-trained apprentice to be elected as convener and was later to go on to become a full-time official for the union and, at the time of writing this, is still working as a full-time official.

A month or so before leaving for Australia, the Ferranti group of companies in the United Kingdom comprising over 14,000 people, seemed to be on the verge of collapse. The government had offered five million pound to tide the group over until the problems were fully investigated and until the government had decided on a long-term policy regarding Ferranti.

Obviously the union members in Edinburgh were concerned about their future. A union delegation from the company, headed by Ernie Leslie and representatives from all unions concerned, went down to a meeting in London. They heard Anthony Wedgwood Benn, the Secretary for Industry, say that he intended to avert the collapse of the company, but he did not give details as to how. I was asked to attend the meeting in London, and I did attend, but I was really a lame duck figure at that time as everyone knew that I was leaving for Australia the following month. I have to say that I felt terrible about leaving when Ferranti was in such a mess. I felt that my experience would have been useful at that time, and at times I felt like a traitor leaving people who I respected and worked with to fight on.

The month before leaving was taken up with packing our furniture for shipment to Brisbane and by selling the items that we were not taking with us. Perhaps the biggest disappointment was that we had to leave some of the boys' toys behind. Roslyn shed a few tears at this.

There was a wonderful dinner and presentation organised by the Shop Stewards' Committee to wish us well and Colin Anderson made a presentation of gifts.

I was also invited to a dinner organised by Eric Mason with himself, Jim McNicol (Mac) and Dougie Rooney at the Gimis International Restaurant in Cockburn Street. I really appreciated the night. We had all been very close as we worked together in our various union jobs and at Ferranti. The meal was best remembered for the wonderful food and the fact that I started a small fire in the restaurant. Whilst reading the menu, I moved a lit candle on the table to near the window and the curtains caught fire. Fortunately the staff put it out. We all joked that if the building had burned down, I would have been sent to Australia, like so many were years before, in a ball and chain. I still have the burnt menu of that evening and it is interesting to note one of the dishes the, 'Specialita Dello Chef' - or Chef's Special - was the Chicken Supreme Breast; 'a half spring chicken cooked in hell'! It was listed at one pound and fifty pence.

We stayed with my cousin Moira and her husband Ian, with whom I had always been close, the night before leaving for Australia. Their two sons Andrew and Gavin stayed with their grandmother that night. In many ways it was surreal for me. It was the last night that I would be spending in Edinburgh. I thought that I would perhaps never set eyes on the city again. It was not a nice feeling. I consoled myself at that time with words similar to the saying, 'You can take the man out of Scotland, but you can't take Scotland out of the man'. I knew that Scotland would always be special to me. I also thought of the wonderful nights that Ian and I had spent over a few pints of beer, times when we discussed politics and Scottish Nationalism and things in general. Whilst we were both poles apart politically we were very good friends. I also remembered the book I read about Robert Louis Stevenson and how, when he left Edinburgh, driving along Princes Street for the last time in his horse-drawn carriage, he did not look back.

The next morning, Ian drove us all to Waverley Station to catch the train to London. On route he turned down opposite Millers Foundry, a route which I believe he took rather than drive past our house and the Artisan Bar where my father and I had spent happy hours together; perhaps he did so to save me from more sadness at the prospect of leaving. By this stage I was trying to be positive and felt that, like Robert Louis Stevenson, it was better to look ahead to the future and not look back.

We made our sad farewells to our friends and family and headed to London on a train and then on to Heathrow Airport and a new and challenging life in Australia.

Winter-time

Late lies the wintry sun a-bed,
A frosty, fiery sleepy-head;
Blinks but an hour or two; and then,
A blood-red orange, sets again.

Before the stars have left the skies,
At morning in the dark I rise;
And shivering in my nakedness,
By the cold candle, bathe and dress.

Close by the jolly fire I sit
To warm my frozen bones a bit;
Or with a reindeer-sled, explore
The colder countries round the door.

When to go out, my nurse doth wrap
Me in my comforter and cap;
The cold wind burns my face, and blows
Its frosty pepper up my nose.

Black are my steps on silver sod;
Thick blows my frosty breath abroad;
And tree and house, and hill and lake,
Are frosted like a wedding cake.

ROBERT LOUIS STEVENSON
(Born November 13, 1850 - Died December 3, 1894)